"Sam Grossman has so much raw energy he has to know a secret. Lucky for us it's a secret no more."

—**Diane Sawyer**

"Sam Grossman and his family practice what they preach, and the results are undeniable. Not only are they trim and fit, but they truly look years younger than their actual age. They have won the food fight and we are so happy he shares his secrets with us in this book."

—**Marianne and Kenny Rogers**

"I've known Sam Grossman for quite a few years and I've always thought it would be wonderful if he would write a book about how to stay fit. Well he did, and it's great. Thank you, Sam."

—**Jimmy Stewart**

"What a delightful book. I'm so pleased to be a part of it. Sam is closing on sixty but acts, thinks, and lives like he's thirty-five. Great common sense, sound judgment, a lot of fun, and a wealth of healthful knowledge."

—**Mariel Hemingway**
Actress, new mother, restaurateur

"This is by far the best bipartisan nutrition plan we've ever seen. If even a quarter of the country would read it and follow Sam's advice, our nation's health-care costs could probably be cut in half . . . a terrific book."

—**Teresa Heinz and**
United States Senator John Heinz

"Sam Grossman has finally given us a sensible diet that is nutritionally sound and really works. He is in excellent physical condition as is his wife, Peggy. . . . Now I know why! . . . Everyone should try it ASAP. . . . By George, you'll love it!"

—**Phyllis George**
Miss America
Emmy Award winner

"Every page is a home run. Sam Grossman knocks the diet fads out of the ballpark and comes to the plate with a witty, timely, and easy way to lose weight, keep it off, stay in shape. *Win the Food Fight* belongs on your kitchen shelf. Don't go to the market without it!"

—Jim Palmer
Baltimore Orioles All-Star Pitcher
Three-time Cy Young Award winner

"Sam orchestrates a perfectly balanced weight-loss program. It's so nutritionally sound, I can't understand why no one has thought of it earlier. Sam's personality shows through in every chapter and makes you smile along the way."

—John Williams
Academy Award–winning composer
Conductor of the Boston Pops

"This is a down-to-earth, no-nonsense, medically sound book. If Sam's advice is taken to heart, liposuction (the most frequently performed plastic surgery operation in America) would be virtually eliminated. With great pleasure I endorse your magnificent book."

—Dr. John Emery
Olympic Gold Medalist
Member, Canadian Sports Hall of Fame

"What this world *does* need is a book that takes the mystery out of nutrition for thinking, working Americans. The beneficial human consequences of following this advice will be around long after several hundred fad diets have come and gone."

—Anthony Frank
Postmaster General of the United States

"I find your book delightful. It is so pragmatic, personal, and engaging—altogether informative and enjoyable and full of practical tips to improve the quality of life for each of us."

—Dr. Thomas D. Rees
Author and Department Chairman
Manhattan Eye, Ear, and Throat Hospital

"If you've ever spent six days white-water kayaking with Sam Grossman, you'll know how faithful he is to the precepts of this book. Simply put, he's living proof that it works—terrifically!"

—**Frank Wells**
President and Chief Operating Officer,
Walt Disney Company

"I've known Sam and his family for more than twenty-five years. This book is the way he really lives. If you want to be fit, trim, and healthy, this is must reading from a winner who will put us all on the Victory Stand."

—**Bobby Beathard**
General Manager,
1988 Super Bowl Champion Washington Redskins

"As a fellow powder-snow nut and physical-fitness buff, Sam has published his ideas (and most of mine) about how to eat and live. Must reading for those who want to lose weight and live a long, healthful life. Bravo, Sam, our prophet for the '90s."

—**John Nordstrom**
Co-Chairman of the Board,
Nordstrom Department Store

"Doctors know about disease but precious little about health. Sam's lifetime experience with eating, living, and weight loss are medically superior. I especially like his comments about oatmeal. I have run thirty-seven marathons and during each one fantasize about eating a huge bowl at the end of the race. Now you can enjoy the same big breakfast, lose weight, and you don't have to run a marathon to do it."

—**Dr. Lynn Levy**
Olympian
Chairman, Sun Valley Sports Medicine Institute

"For anyone from ironman triathletes to professional football players to couch potatoes, Sam's book has an enlightening and essential message on good exercise and nutrition. Sam has also accomplished what up until now has been impossible—making a book on nutrition and exercise very entertaining reading."

—**Pat Bowlen**
President and Chief Executive Officer,
Denver Broncos Football Club

"Sam's insights into diet, health, and exercise are well worth reading—even the most knowledgeable reader will find some new 'pearls.' "

—**Thom Weisel**
President of the United States Ski Team

"Sam Grossman delivers a ONE-TWO PUNCH to America's midriff bulge. *Win the Food Fight* is the battle plan for a longer, stronger, thinner win. BUY THIS BOOK!"

—**Harvey Mackay**
Author of *Swim with the Sharks Without Being Eaten Alive*

"I've researched every diet program for a decade and this book is laser accurate . . . truly the BEST. Full of common-sense brilliance and real-life examples, it melts away the fitness fallacies along with our excess fat. Read, underline, and share this book with everyone you love."

—**Dr. Denis Waitley**
U.S. Olympic Sports Medicine Council

"My whole life has been involved with athletics, health, nutrition, and exercise. I heartily recommend Sam's book to athletes and nonathletes alike. Everyone will benefit from this sound advice."

—**O. J. Simpson**

"Sam Grossman is the best advertisement for his book. He and his whole family are fit, energetic, and healthy. . . . Who wouldn't want his secret!"

—**Maria Shriver**

"We ought to put Sam Grossman in charge of eliminating the federal deficit. *Win the Food Fight* clearly shows the way to cut excess fat!"

—**Ed Muskie**
Secretary of State
U.S. Senator
Governor of Maine

"Sam Grossman's *Win the Food Fight* is an important addition to physical fitness. It is a carefully researched and sound guideline for nutrition and exercise that will benefit each of us in our quest for feeling and looking better."

—**Roger Staubach**

"Sam's book is insightful reading. His message is worth learning for everyone interested in a healthy lifestyle. There are some great lessons in Sam's easy style."

—**Peter Ueberroth**

"*Win the Food Fight* sings like a song to me. Sam has written the *must* nutrition book for the nineties."

—**Barbra Streisand**

"Sam Grossman is a nice boy. Why he wants to put all the delicatessens in this country out of business is beyond me."

—**Jackie Mason**

WIN
T · H · E
FOOD
FIGHT
The 7-Week Victory Diet

WIN THE FOOD FIGHT

The 7-Week Victory Diet

Sam Grossman

St. Martin's Press ■ New York

NOTE TO READER

No single diet can be ideal for every individual. Anyone having a suspected medical condition or taking any medication that might be affected by diet or exercise should consult a physician before undertaking this or any other diet or exercise program. Be certain to ask the physician, however, if he or she has training in or knowledge of nutrition, fitness, and exercise.

This diet and program are the result of the author's research and experience. Neither the publisher nor the author makes any warranty, express or implied, with respect to this book or its contents, and neither is or shall be liable for any claims arising from use of or reliance upon this book.

Library of Congress
Cataloging-in-Publication Data

Grossman, Sam.
    Win the food fight.

    1. Reducing diets—Recipes. I. Title.
RM222.2.G75   1989   613.2'5   89-4073
ISBN 0-312-02988-8

Design by Judith A. Stagnitto

First Edition
10 9 8 7 6 5 4 3 2 1

For Peggy, the world's best-looking thirty-year-old (who happens to be fifty!), and for our three sensational kids: Jimmy, Courtney, and John

CONTENTS

WINNER'S CIRCLE PROFILES

WHY SAM KNOWS WHAT HE'S TALKING ABOUT

by Dr. David Sime

Author's Note: Dave Sime is much too modest, so I would like to acknowledge that he is not only a world-renowned physician and surgeon but also a world-class athlete. In addition to winning an Olympic silver medal, Dave at one time held seven world records, and held the world record for the 200-yard dash for ten years. He was All-American in baseball and track in the same season and was drafted by the Detroit Lions football team. He opted for medical school where he graduated AOA (the equivalent of Phi Beta Kappa) from Duke University.

hen I was a medical student thirty years ago, most college and university programs offered precious little in the way of nutritional training. If you had an interest in the subject—as I did—you had to learn it on your own. That's why I read every nutrition and diet book I could find.

My interest was twofold. As a doctor-to-be, I wanted to have a thorough knowledge of the important role good nutrition plays in maintaining good health. As an athlete who had an eye on making the U.S. Olympic track team, I knew that good eating habits would be just as important as good exercise and training habits. I developed my own nutritional program by eating basic, wholesome meals. It paid off. In 1960 I won a silver medal at the Rome games, and for a number of years I held several world track records.

In the years that followed I kept up my good eating habits, and so did my family. I also kept up my interest in nutrition, continuing to read as many diet books as possible. So I was more than a little interested when I met Sam Grossman, his wife, and his family on a rafting trip in Idaho.

At only a glance, I knew Sam and his family were in great shape. I've learned in medicine to gauge a person's health quite literally by looking at the eyes. For example, I am able to judge fairly accurately the amount of cholesterol-related plaque in a person's system by glancing at the blood vessels in the eyes. When I looked in Sam's, it was obvious I was seeing a very fit man in the prime of life. That's why I was astonished when he told me he was almost sixty years old.

And Sam's wife, Peggy, was one of the best-looking fifty-year-old women I'd ever seen. Sam told me that after three children she looked better in a bikini than she did when they were married twenty-six years earlier.

I asked Sam how he and Peggy managed it, and that's when I learned of his thirty-year interest in nutrition and health. He told me how he runs health fairs at his shopping centers and how he has conducted surveys at those centers to learn the eating habits of Americans. He told me how, on the basis of this research, he had developed his own easy-to-follow health plan that had helped dozens of people in his company to lose weight. He also told me how he was finishing a book about his weight-loss and health ideas.

I told Sam that when he had finished his book I wanted to read it. Well, I've just finished the manuscript and, simply put, my reaction is . . . "Finally!"

Win the Food Fight offers the most common-sense information and advice of any diet and nutrition book I've read. It will not only help you lose weight; it will also help you gain health and gain control over your eating habits. In fact, all the eating habits supported in this book fit within the latest scientific and medical opinions outlined in the Surgeon General's 1988 Report on Nutrition and Health.

There's even more good news: Once you've followed the initial 11-in-7 Strategy, and have reached "the Winner's Circle," achieving what Sam calls your target weight, then Sam shows you how to design your own plan that will have you eating from your own repertoire of favorite meals.

When I got to that part of Sam's book, I had to smile, because what Sam recommends is very similar to the eating habits I developed to help me set a number of world records. I was also pleased to find that my habits are similar to those of the celebrities Sam has profiled in this book. All these people have achieved permanent fitness and good health by eating from a few favorite recipes that are low in fat, cholesterol, and salt, and high in fiber and other nutritive benefits. Each has reached the Winner's Circle of good health and vibrant energy.

But none of these people—including me—had the benefit of an easy-to-follow plan to help them get where they are now. That's why I believe this book is so important. That's why I believe the Victory Diet that you will find in this book will change the way America eats.

INTRODUCTION

WHY YOU SHOULD READ THIS BOOK

I'm a businessman who has built a very successful company that specializes in real estate investment, development, construction, leasing, and management. I did it with no formal business training, using common sense to help me make decisions.

So how does that qualify me to write a book on nutrition and exercise? Because during the time I've worked to build my company, I've also worked on my parallel interest in nutrition and exercise. I've learned that you don't need to go to business school to be a successful entrepreneur, and *you don't need to be a doctor to develop nutrition and exercise habits that are easy to follow and that keep you trim and healthy*.

The 7-Week Victory Diet is based on my three decades of interest in nutrition, exercise, and the dietary habits of people all over the world. The single most important rule that I've learned in these thirty years is that to be successful, a weight-loss and health plan has to be simple and easy. That's why in this book there is none of that nonsense of Day 1, Breakfast A, Lunch B, Dinner C; Day 2, Breakfast D, Lunch E, Dinner F; Day 3, and so on. This kind of schedule makes shopping for groceries as taxing as taking a college chemistry course. I've learned that losing weight doesn't need to involve complicated menu plans. I've learned that there is no reason to waste time searching grocery aisles with a long shopping list of exotic ingredients that then take hours to prepare.

My plan is for people who don't have time for diets. On the Victory Diet you eat from only eleven basic menus and follow a plan that you can fully embrace in only seven weeks. That's why I call it the 11-in-7 Strategy.

But how can you eat from only eleven basic menus without getting bored? The answer: You can do it because, as shown by my research, if you are like most other people *you already eat from about a dozen basic recipes. In other words, you may be halfway toward embracing my plan and not even know it.*

The only thing you may have to do to achieve permanent weight loss is simply substitute the foods and menus suggested in this book for your current diet. You may not have to deny yourself anything but a few old eating habits that you probably won't miss anyway.

My plan works because it is not a restrictive diet plan. It works because I've learned that losing weight and keeping it off have nothing to do with starvation, misery, and denial. Any diet or exercise plan built around any of these three oppressors is doomed to failure.

By following the *Win the Food Fight* Victory Diet you can eat just about all you want. And when it comes to breakfast, the Victory Diet in this book says you *should* eat as much as you can. On this plan, breakfast becomes the foundation of each day, the pattern for the rest of your meals.

And what is that Victory Breakfast? It's a cereal so nutritious and beneficial to your health that if it didn't already exist,

I'm certain some white-coated lab technician would invent it and make a fortune on the patent. It's a cereal that guards against colon disease such as diverticulosis (which affects 50 percent of all Americans over fifty!) and reduces your chance of heart attack. It's a cereal that keeps you regular and consequently helps you lose weight. It's a cereal that I call The Incredible Shrinking Machine.

What is this wonder food? *It's good old oatmeal.*

Now, I know a lot of you just said to yourself, wait a minute, nobody can convince me to eat oatmeal five or six days a week for the rest of my life. But if you read on, my evidence will convince you that you *can* eat oatmeal nearly every day and love it.

I'll show you that, if you are like most other people, you *already* eat the same breakfast nearly every day anyway, and that's why it will be easy to trade your current breakfast habit for the oatmeal Victory Breakfast habit.

I'll show you why you need to eat as much for breakfast as possible, and why the more you eat for breakfast, the more weight you will lose!

My plan shows how eating a big breakfast sets you up to eat the right-sized lunch and dinner, guaranteeing that you won't "pig out" later in the day. On the *7-Week Victory Diet* you'll learn to eat as the old saying suggests:

> Eat breakfast like a king,
> Lunch like a prince,
> Dinner like a pauper!

Learning to eat from eleven basic menus for breakfast, lunch, and dinner is only half of the Victory Diet. The other half is adopting an easy and enjoyable exercise routine that takes just ten minutes a day and keeps your stomach toned, helps you stand straight, and puts a bounce back in your walk.

On the Victory Diet, you can be on your way to permanent weight loss, on your way to conquering the constant battle against overeating, on your way to a longer and stronger life, in only seven weeks. That's no idle claim, either. It's based on the many case histories of people in my company who have achieved permanent weight loss by following the Victory Diet. Not only have they changed their eating habits in seven weeks, but a few people who were as much as forty pounds overweight have also reached their target weights—the ideal weight for their individual height and body shape—in that time. The Victory Diet works for them, and it will work for you.

◄ Part I ►

WINNING THE FOOD FIGHT

Your Fat Days Are Over

It's sobering to realize how pervasive is the lack of nutritional knowledge in our country. I once participated in a tour of the U.S. Naval Academy at Annapolis, Maryland. I had an intimate look at the academy, viewing the grounds, classrooms, science labs, and computer rooms. I was impressed—everything was first cabin. Then I had lunch with the cadets, and my level of esteem for their operation dropped several notches. In fact, I was appalled at the greasy bacon, canned fruit salad, white bread, and chocolate sundaes. In an afternoon question-and-answer session with the academy's commandant, I voiced my dismay. He thought I was joking. "The Navy food is just good ol' standard American cooking," he said with a grin.

He was right. It was just good ol' standard American cooking, but the Standard American Diet (read that as S.A.D.) is nothing to smile about. It's no way to feed the Navy, and it's no way to feed the rest of us. The Standard American Diet—overfilled with fats and underfilled with nutrients and fiber—is the reason 80 million people in this country are overweight.

The Standard American Diet is also one of the leading causes of disease in our country. What most Americans eat not only contributes to heaviness, but also shortens one's life span. The 1988 Surgeon General's *Report on Nutrition and Health* says, "Diseases of dietary excess and imbalance . . . now rank among the leading causes of illness and death in the United States." If you're still unconvinced, consider these facts:

- After reviewing years of research on the subject of nutrition, the National Academy of Sciences concluded that *60 percent of the cancer in men and 40 percent in women is related to diet*.

- Studies have shown that there is *a very strong link between obesity and the risk of diabetes*.

- A recent study testing 92,898 men found that a diet high in fat (in other words, the Standard American Diet) increased the risk of colon cancer by 63 percent and the risk of rectal cancer by 70 percent.

- The National Research Council concluded that of the ten major leading causes of death in the United States, *at least 50 percent were related to lifestyle factors*. And most of those factors had to do with the Standard American Diet.

When I first started collecting facts like these, I had no doubt that one of the most important things I could do for myself and my family was to develop an easy-to-follow nutrition and exercise plan that would keep us trim and give us longer and stronger lives.

What I found was that "easy-to-follow" plans were not necessarily easy to figure out. It took about thirty years of reading journals, books, and articles, and thinking about the subject of nutrition. But in that time I finally discovered that the way to stay trim and fit and the way to gain easy, permanent control over excess eating is really a rediscovery of what our grandparents and ancestors knew all along: The secret is to eat from a few basic recipes, to eat as big a breakfast as you can hold, and to eat mostly fiber-rich complex carbohydrates. Then add to that a few simple, low-volume exercises—just ten minutes a day—and your fat days are over.

Why Did I Write This Book, Anyway?

One morning not long ago I was walking through one of my shopping malls when I passed an electronics store with ten big TV sets tuned to the same station. I stopped in fascination to watch the identical headshots of overweight women discuss their fate:

The first woman put Suzie Qs on the dashboard of her car in the sun so they would get moldy. Three or four times a week she'd try to eat them in order to eliminate her desire for sweets.

The ten TVs were tuned to a popular talk show. The woman who spoke those words was obviously at wits' end. The next lady sounded even more desperate. She was addicted to diet pills. When those failed, she would eat all she wanted, then make herself vomit.

I listened as more guests described their dietary woes.

One woman complained that when she went into a department store, the clerks made her feel like she just wasn't there. Another confessed that getting on a crowded bus and looking for a seat was pure hell. One mother confided that she had put her daughter on diet pills when she was twelve because she didn't like having a fat child. After a time, the daughter became addicted.

One of the men on the show expressed depression about eating in front of people because, even if he was eating a diet meal, people would look at him as though he were pigging out. The final person to speak was a woman who said that she often got whistles from men as she was driving, but that the whistles stopped when she got out of the car.

I walked back to my office imagining how traumatic and humiliating it must be for an overweight person to do something like go into a store and buy a bathing suit, let alone wear it in public. If only he or she knew how easy it can be to win the food fight! With the talk show people still on my mind, I looked around at everyone in my office and noticed that quite a few people *there* were overweight, too. I had worked with many of these people for ten years or more, and yet in a way I had never *seen* them. Some were just like the people on the TV show, and I realized that they must have the same stories of frustration and despair.

If only *these* people knew how easy it was! If only they knew that changing their breakfast-eating habits alone would do wonders toward slimming them down!

Then it occurred to me that maybe I could show them. Maybe I could get some of these people in my office to replace whatever it was they were eating with some of the simple eating habits that had kept my family and me in great health for most of our lives.

That led me to wonder just what it was that many people did eat on a regular basis. To find out, I sent a questionnaire to the people in my office. Their answers weren't surprising. The diets of most of them were high in fat and low in complex carbohydrates. Most people ate large quantities of red meat and often indulged in packaged foods dripping with saturated oils and fat. The fact that intrigued me most, however, was that 75 *percent of the people who answered the questionnaire ate the same thing every day for breakfast*. They ate from a very limited set of basic recipes for lunch and dinner, too.

I was fascinated with that statistic, because eating from a few basic menus was the core of my own nutrition plan. That gave me an idea. If everyone was already eating the same thing for breakfast at least five days a week, could they be convinced to substitute a healthy breakfast for their fat-laden one? If they ate the same breakfast every day anyway, it shouldn't be too hard to get them to eat from either of two easy-to-fix breakfast menus that I had developed over the years.

If they could make this one substitution and make it part of their lifestyle, then the next step—substituting healthy lunches and dinners—might be easier.

It sounded like a good plan, but just how was I going to get everybody to substitute new habits for their old ones? To a businessman, the answer seemed obvious: Pay them to do it!

Such an incentive program would be a good investment, I reasoned. Many progressive companies have installed gyms and health programs. These outfits know that lean and fit people get more work done because they have more energy, and they have fewer sick days and medical bills because they are healthier. Why not try it with my own company?

I drafted a memo outlining my diet plan and the incentive: Everyone who adopted the eating plan would receive $5 for every pound he or she lost and kept off. The offer would last two months. We would have three weigh-ins: when we started, at the end of the first month, and the final one at the end of the second month. At that time, anybody who had regained any of the weight he or she had lost had to return $5 per pound regained.

Twenty-one people signed up: fifteen women and six men. At the end of the first month, the group had lost a total of 167 pounds. I shelled out $835. At the end of the second month, the group had lost another thirty-one pounds, so I paid out $155. At the final weigh-in, two people had each regained two pounds, so I got back $20.

The money turned out to be well invested. People lost weight and kept it off. They were all comfortable with their new habits within seven weeks. Some individuals lost as much as forty pounds. They said the plan was easy to follow and that they most liked its lack of restrictions. In fact, on my plan they were encouraged to eat all they could hold for breakfast!

More memos followed, with advice on how to eat in restaurants and how to get through the holiday season without pigging out too badly. Several people were interested in exercise programs, and their requests generated even more memos. When it was suggested that I write a book, I looked at the stack of memos and at my office full of newly healthy employees and decided that the idea wasn't a bad one. These employees were living proof that I had a plan that worked. And everybody said how easy it was to follow. I decided to take a shot at it.

To create a book, I realized that I would need a broader base than my office staff. I would need more information about people's eating habits. For many years the shopping malls my company owns and manages in conjunction with Phoenix Children's Hospital, St. John's Hospital, Phoenix Baptist Hospital, and the Maricopa County Health Association had sponsored health fairs, seminars, and clinics designed to teach people better eating and health-care habits. That gave me the idea to use one mall for a survey to learn the dietary habits of a sample pool of shoppers. By surveying a cross section of the forty thousand people who passed through the mall on a typical weekend day, I felt I would obtain a fair reflection of the eating habits of most Americans. The results of this survey were nearly identical to the results of the survey conducted at my office. I can sum up the results in two sentences:

If you're an average American, the chances are that you eat from just a few basic recipes.

If you're an average American, the chances are that you eat the same (usually lousy) breakfast at least five days a week.

Here is just a sample of the questions asked, and the responses.

	YES (%)	NO (%)
Do you consider yourself overweight?	45	55
Have you ever been on a diet?	77	23
Did you regain the weight?	79	21
Do you eat basically the same breakfast at least five days a week?	73	27
Do you eat the same lunch at least three days a week?	42	58
Do you eat the same dinner at least three days a week?	60	40

How many nights a week do you eat red meat?

Two	42 percent
Four	38 percent
Seven	13 percent
None	7 percent

I decided to come up with the Victory Diet for winning the food fight based on this knowledge that the majority of Americans eat from just a few basic recipes. It seemed obvious to me that diet books advocating complicated diets with dozens and dozens of recipes were missing the point. Why not create a nutrition plan that could help people achieve permanent weight loss by simply substituting a few new eating habits for a few old ones?

I hope it's also obvious that I'm not going to pay you $5 for every pound you lose. After you read this book, you won't need any additional motivation to start changing your eating and exercise habits. In fact, losing weight on the Victory Diet and permanently winning the food fight are so elementary, so easy, so enjoyable, that there's a good chance you'll start on the diet even before you finish the book.

◄ ◄ 2 ► ►

Two Health
Hazards: Doctors
and Fad Diets

made my success in business
by following my own common sense. I didn't go to business
school, and I don't have an M.B.A. Not that higher education
isn't valuable, but I believe my own example shows that good
common sense can often get you just as far.

The same is true for nutrition, exercise, and diet. In the
previous chapter I mentioned how I taught myself good eating
and good exercise habits. I did my own research. I had many
lengthy discussions with several doctor friends who are very
knowledgeable about nutrition. I read dozens and dozens of
books, magazine articles, and journals.

I learned enough to develop what I am convinced is a plan
that will work for everyone. But I also learned, after a number
of dead ends and false leads, that for anyone trying to learn
about nutrition and health there are two potential pitfalls you

must avoid: doctors who know little about nutrition, and diets and diet books that are based more on conjecture than nutrition.

The Doctor Doesn't Always Know Best

If you put 100 doctors in a room and ask them what they recommend for a ruptured appendix, almost all will respond, "Remove it surgically." If you put the same doctors in a room and tell them Mrs. Jones is twenty-five pounds overweight, and ask them what to do, you'd probably get close to 100 different opinions.

If you don't believe me, consider this: A 1983 federal survey found that 40 percent of the doctors in the United States did not counsel their patients to change their eating habits until their cholesterol levels reached 300 or higher! A 1987 study showed that doctors in the United States advise fewer than half their patients who smoke to quit, even the ones who are overweight and have high blood pressure!

It's little wonder that doctors are in the dark about nutrition and health. A recent Senate-subcommittee investigation revealed that the average U.S. physician gets only about *three hours* of training in nutrition out of *four years* of medical school.

There are some doctors who acknowledge this shortcoming. Dr. Roy Walford, professor of pathology at UCLA and noted author of *The 120-Year Diet*, four other books, and more than 250 scientific articles, says, "Nutrition is still a woefully insignificant part of the medical school curriculum. Doctors are apt to feel safe in hiding their ignorance of the subject behind their doctoral authority. That's not what you want."

I couldn't agree more. That's why if you consult a doctor about diet, nutrition, and exercise, you would be smart to ask first if he or she has any substantial knowledge about the subject. Consider, for example, what happened to a management executive at my company who tried to get some meaningful nutrition advice from some of the leading family physicians in her area.

A Management Executive's Visit to the Doctors

When I started working on this book, Martha was about forty pounds overweight. You'll recall the offer I made to my employees to pay them $5 for every pound lost while following my program. Initially, Martha hesitated to take me up on the offer, but as she helped on this manuscript, she got more interested and finally decided to give it a shot.

That gave me an idea. For some time I had been suspicious about the kind of nutritional advice people get from their doctors. What if before starting my plan Martha went to three doctors in our area and asked them what they thought about losing weight?

Martha agreed to the proposal. She promised not to give away the fact that she was working on a nutrition book. She said she would go for an appointment and ask each doctor the same thing: "How can I lose forty pounds?" She did a little research and found three doctors in family practice who had good reputations as long-established Phoenix physicians.

Doctor #1

Doctor #1 first asked Martha about her health history, her lifestyle, and her eating and exercise patterns. He then talked to her about behavior modification (he didn't explain what he meant by that) and the need to make time to exercise and eat properly (he didn't explain anything about the amount of time or what kind of exercise, or what kind of food to eat). When she asked him about a specific diet, he told her the Rotation Diet was good. He warned that it would not work quickly, and that if she was really interested in losing weight and keeping it off, she should not look for any miracle solutions. When Martha arrived, a nurse had taken her blood pressure, but the doctor didn't take any blood for an analysis (or arrange for her to come back in the morning, before eating, when blood samples are usually taken). He didn't give her any kind of physical. He didn't even weigh her! The visit lasted ten minutes and cost her $35.

Doctor #2

Doctor #2 kept Martha waiting for forty-five minutes. The entire interview lasted no more than three minutes. He said, "You should get more exercise and eat less." Again, there was no suggestion of a blood test, weighing, stress test, physical, or any plan even remotely based on medical science. The three-minute visit cost $25.

Doctor #3

Doctor #3 kept Martha waiting for thirty minutes and then spent three minutes telling her approximately what Doctor #2 had told her but also suggesting that if she was interested he could prescribe some diet pills. Cost: $25.

I think Martha's experience shows pretty clearly that when seeking nutritional advice from a doctor, it is wise to shop around. That's not to say you can't find good doctors who are knowledgeable about nutrition and health and who can offer sound advice. But it's "buyer beware."

The same is true with nutrition books, especially fad diet books. Many of them contain no more useful advice than that provided by the three doctors Martha visited.

Beware the Fad Diet

Ernest Hemingway once said, "The most essential quality for a good writer is a built-in, shock-proof shit detector." He could have said the same thing for a concerned individual trying to find a good diet book. I'm convinced there is more baloney (if you'll pardon the expression) masquerading under the banner of "diet" than under any subject in popular American culture.

Just consider the names of some of the diets recently promoted in books and magazine articles: The Inner Thigh Diet, The Dare-to-Bare Diet, The Drinking Man's Diet, The Light Beer Diet: Brew Away 5 Pounds Fast, The Anti-Hangover Diet.

Some sound pretty upper crust: The Beverly Hills Diet, The Scarsdale Diet, The Southampton Diet. Others are more middle crust: The Nashville Meltdown Diet, The Texas Miracle Diet.

Roseanne Barr, the wonderfully funny, fat comedienne, describes the highly effective Mirror Diet, on which you eat all of your meals nude in front of a mirror. She complains, however, that most good restaurants refuse to go for it.

Americans aren't the only victims of diet gimmicks. A weight-loss clinic in Bangkok recently instructed patients to jam ten lettuce seeds into their ears before eating in order to reduce their appetites. The treatment was cheap, but the clinic warned patients to replace the seeds every two weeks "or they might soften and germinate."

One of the more successful diet fads of recent years advocates eating fruit for breakfast. This diet says that from the time you wake up in the morning until at least noon you should consume nothing but fresh fruit and fruit juice. Along with many qualified nutritionists and nutrition writers such as Jane Brody, I am unequivocally opposed to that idea. The authors of this diet say, "A heavy breakfast means a heavy day. A light breakfast means a light, vibrant day."

Where I come from, we call statements like that P.R.—B.S. A light breakfast of only fruit and juice won't get you anything but an empty tank by about 10:30 in the morning. And if by midmorning you do have any gas in your tank, it won't be the kind that will give you extra energy. I'm not saying eating only fruit until noon is bad for you, but I am saying it won't get the job done. Morning is when you are switching from your rest cycle to your active cycle. Your core temperature, energy output, and hormone production are all down, and you absolutely need a nutritious breakfast to get into an active mode.

Despite this weakness, the success of this diet has made the authors the weight-loss gurus of the 1980s. Naturally they followed their hit with a sequel book. In it they maintain that anything overdone suffers in quality. Disneyland once in a while is fun, they say, but too often and you get sick of it. Same for sex.

Whoooaaa! Disneyland and sex? Give me a break!

So you have to approach the advice of many diet books with caution. There are some very good ones out there, however. Probably the best is Jane Brody's *Good Food Book*. It has some terrific recipes, and her nutritional information is right on the money. Robert Haas's *Eat to Win* is also good. The only thing about it I fault is that the program is very complicated and strict. The same is true for the Pritikin program.

I hope it's clear why it's important for you to teach yourself the basics of nutrition. The 1988 Surgeon General's *Report on Nutrition and Health* is a good starting point. If you've got a *serious* weight problem and think you should consult a physician, call around and find one who really knows about nutrition and exercise.

◄ ◄ 3 ► ►

Why You Should Become Your Own "Health Celebrity"

At the same time I was conducting the shopping mall survey, I had the idea to send a questionnaire to several dozen friends, acquaintances, and friends of friends to learn about their eating habits. Many of these people—such as Mariel Hemingway, Jim Palmer, and Clint Eastwood—are very successful in business, sports, or the entertainment field, and I thought it might be interesting and fun to see what they ate.

When their questionnaires came back, I was fascinated to learn that most of these people—no matter how well-known or rich or powerful—eat from only a few basic recipes. These are people who could dine out every day at the Ritz, yet nearly every one has chosen to eat the same breakfast at least five days a week, and centers other eating habits around a few favorite lunch and dinner menus.

Although these people eat simple meals, they also enjoy healthy meals. No matter how busy and hectic their schedules, they find time to eat nutritious foods and get daily exercise. And they are all at or near their target weights—the ideal weight in relation to body shape and size.

In going through these questionnaires, I realized that most of the eating habits of these people aren't much different from what I'd discovered works for me and my family and what I used as the core for developing *The 7-Week Victory Diet*.

Many of these people, for example, eat high-fiber cereals for breakfast nearly every day, and they have a low-fat lunch and dinner selected from a small repertoire of favorite recipes. Most of them don't drink coffee or hard liquor, and the majority don't eat red meat. And none of them smoke.

I also learned that most of them have developed an interesting balance to keep their eating and exercise habits in equilibrium. If, for example, someone's schedule temporarily forces him or her into an abuse of exercise habits, the person is often more careful to follow healthy eating habits. I was fascinated to see how each individual compensates for his or her own erratic schedule in planning meals and exercise workouts. Clearly these people had long ago learned to conquer the food fight, and their good habits were a natural part of a busy, successful lifestyle.

How did these people arrive at personal plans that worked for them? I learned that nearly all of them had developed their plans on their own. Nearly all of them were the types who had their antennae tuned and ready to pick up new ideas. They would read a snippet in the *Wall Street Journal* about a study that shows oatmeal lowers serum cholesterol, and they would decide to eat oatmeal for breakfast. They would see a sidebar in a news magazine saying broccoli has been shown to contain anticarcinogens, and they would make it a point to eat broccoli twice a week. A friend would explain they would be better off eating less red meat, and another would tell them potatoes and pasta don't make you fat. They would decide to take a walk every evening, swim laps at the pool on Tuesdays and Thursdays, and get a bicycle for weekend outings. It would take a while, but eventually they would get enough new habits, and lo and behold, they would stay slim and fit.

Since many of the ideas these people had devised were parallel to my own plan, I have included profiles of eighteen of them throughout the book and have called them Winner's Circle Profiles.

You'll also notice that even though all these people eat healthy food, several of them have eating habits that do not exactly follow the 11-in-7 Strategy—the first part of the Victory Diet.

Don't let that confuse you. The reason these people vary slightly from the 11-in-7 Strategy is because they have arrived at their personal plans after years of experimentation, and their plans work for them. The Victory Diet allows you to devise your own personal program.

As I'll show you later in the book, once you reach your target weight by following the 11-in-7 Strategy, you can create your personal repertoire of eleven favorite menus—eleven health menus—so that you can enjoy a lifetime of trim and fit eating habits, like the people in the Winner's Circle Profiles.

First, however, you have to learn to replace your old eating habits with new eating habits, and the most effective way to do that is to follow a specific, step-by-step plan.

That's why it is essential for you to follow the main part of the 11-in-7 Strategy. The next section—Part II—will show you *why* it's important to eat only from the following:

Two basic breakfast menus
Four basic lunch menus
Five basic dinner menus

Part III will show you why it's important for you to go through a morning low-volume exercise routine that takes only ten minutes.

Part IV will show you *how* to acquire the habit of eating from your eleven basic menus and of following your low-volume exercise routine *in only seven weeks*.

Then once these new (good) habits become old (good) habits, you can watch the pounds disappear. And once you reach your target weight—the ideal weight for your body shape and size, which I'll show you how to determine later in the book—you'll be ready for Part V, where I explain some basics of nutrition that will guide you in developing a maintenance plan that will have you eating from your own repertoire of favorite menus.

So if you're sick and tired of waging the food fight against overeating and excess pounds; if you're sick and tired of complicated, restrictive diets, then turn the page and start reading, because your fat days are over.

◄ Part II ►

THE VICTORY
NUTRITION
PLAN

Jim Palmer

Jim Palmer is probably best known for his work as a sportscaster for ABC-TV, and for those dynamite ads for Jockey underwear. Others will remember him as a three-time Cy Young Award winner and as All-Star pitcher for the Baltimore Orioles.

Age: 41
Weight at 21: 210 pounds
Weight today: 190 pounds

BREAKFAST

Four days a week Jim has orange juice or half a grapefruit; oatmeal; a few raisins; one slice whole-wheat toast; no coffee; no tea. The balance of the week for breakfast he eats seven-grain cereal.

LUNCH

Jim rarely eats lunch, but when he does it's usually tuna salad.

DINNER

The usual dinner four days a week is pasta with very light dressing such as melted margarine, garlic, and some grated cheese; a green salad; a glass of wine. Other days he eats a salad followed by fish or chicken with vegetables, and rice or potatoes. He tries to eat dinner by 6:30 P.M. no matter where he is. He never eats dessert, but as a snack he enjoys popcorn without butter and salt.

Jim likes to cook (in fact, when he stays at our home, he takes over the kitchen), and has a knockout chicken recipe, which I've included on page 76.

EXERCISE

Jim works out thirty to forty-five minutes, five days a week, even when he broadcasts the World Series, by bicycling or playing volley-ball, tennis, or racquetball. I don't know if you've seen Jim in the Jockey ads, but if you haven't, take a look. He's a perfect example of how eating from a careful selection of basic, healthy menus, combined with daily exercise, will give you a trim and healthy body that opens the door to a successful and vital life.

Eat Breakfast like a King—*What* You Need to Eat

The Victory Breakfast: Foundation of Your Day

Breakfast is the most maligned meal. People ignore it, brush it off, think they can get by without it. From the time we are kids, we're surrounded by the wrong information about breakfast. For example, we may believe the following:

1. If you eat a big breakfast, you are going to eat big and feel big for the rest of the day.
2. Whole-grain cereals make you fat.
3. Bacon and eggs are the best way to start your day.
4. Coffee and toast for breakfast is the way to lose weight.

All four are breakfast myths. All four should be replaced with the single overriding truth about breakfast:

Breakfast is the most important meal of your day.

Morning is the time your body is coming out of its rest cycle and starting its active cycle. Studies have shown that in the morning your body's core temperature is down as much as two degrees. Your pulse is often ten beats or so lower than during the height of your active phase. Your hormonal production is also down.

The evidence is conclusive that what you need in the morning more than anything is energy to get your body out of its rest cycle, and that means you need the Victory Breakfast.

The Two Tenets of the Victory Breakfast

The Victory Breakfast is based on two guiding principles distilled from my own experience and my research of the breakfast habits of people nationwide.

1. On *The 7-Week Victory Diet* you eat the same kind of breakfast every day. Specifically, every day you select either an oatmeal breakfast menu or a whole-grain cold-cereal breakfast menu.

2. On *The 7-Week Victory Diet* you eat a very big breakfast: at least one—even two—large bowls of oatmeal or cold cereal. Your first reaction may be that this sounds crazy, but in the next chapter I'll show how eating a large breakfast will actually help you to lose weight *and* gain life-long health.

Before I explain the *why*, however, I want to spend this chapter telling you the *what*. I want to show you *what* the two delicious meals are that you will be eating on the Victory Breakfast.

> ## *The Oatmeal Victory Breakfast*
>
> *Half a Grapefruit*
>
> *One large serving Hot Oatmeal*
> *with Skim Milk,*
> *a few Raisins, and dash of Cinnamon*
>
> *One slice Whole-Grain Toast*
> *(Add a small amount of margarine if you wish)*
>
> *1 cup Herbal Tea*
> *or (if you must)*
> *1 cup Coffee or Regular Tea*

Oatmeal: The Real Breakfast of Champions

Stated simply, there is no other readily available breakfast cereal as good for you as oatmeal. Consider these facts:

1. Oatmeal is nonfattening. It contains fewer than 100 calories per one-cup serving.
2. Oatmeal is inexpensive. It costs about 13¢ per serving.

3. Oatmeal has a very healthy balance of carbohydrate, protein, and fat. Here's the breakdown of a one-cup serving:

	Grams	Percentage of total calories
Carbohydrate	23	68
Protein	5	15
Fat	3	18*

*Gram for gram, fat has about twice as many calories as either carbohydrates or proteins.

4. Oatmeal actually helps lower your serum cholesterol level. While no one is certain exactly how this works, scientists suspect it's because oatmeal helps your body to filter bile acids that otherwise would linger in your system and act as agents in the manufacture of more cholesterol. Eating oatmeal or oat bran can actually increase your body's ability to excrete bile acid as much as 50 percent and it's no surprise that a few doctors who have read reports of recent studies on oatmeal and oat bran recommend it to patients with hazardously high cholesterol levels.

5. Oatmeal tastes great. I know I may get some initial resistance here, but I guarantee that if you eat the moderate-sized Victory Dinner early in the evening, you'll wake up hungry, and oatmeal will taste fantastic.

There's been a lot of hoopla on oat bran, and while it's true that oat bran contains about twice as much fiber as oatmeal, it is much less appealing and much less versatile for recipes. By itself it's not as satisfying or filling as oatmeal and, in fact, many people think oat bran tastes like wet sand.

Researchers say, however, that oat products in general and oatmeal in particular have the same benefit as oat bran, and that eating a large amount of oatmeal (which I recommend in the Victory Breakfast) is just as effective as eating the usual-sized serving of oat bran.

If you feel you want to eat oat bran but don't like the taste, sprinkle some in with your oatmeal. That way you'll cover all your bases.

But I Haven't Got Time to Cook Oatmeal

This is just what it sounds like—an excuse. The Oatmeal Victory Breakfast takes about as much time to prepare as you would spend turning on the TV to catch the morning weather report. You can have it cooked and on the table ready to eat in less than five minutes. And we're not talking about instant or "one-minute" oatmeal but the good, old-fashioned regular style rolled oats (such as Quaker Oats) that you can buy in every grocery store in the United States.

Here's how you do it:

1. Look at your watch and note the time. To start the oatmeal, combine 1½ cups water with ½ cup oatmeal and set on the stove, uncovered, at high heat. *Do not* salt the water; the oatmeal will taste fine without it. Now put your tea water on to boil.
2. While you wait for everything to come to a boil, slice the grapefruit, put a slice of bread in the toaster, and a tea bag in your mug.
3. After the oatmeal has boiled, stir it and let it boil for three to four minutes, stirring occasionally. Then turn the heat to low and put the lid on the pot.
4. Pour the other boiling water over your teabag. Then take the toast out, spread it with a little safflower-oil margarine or fruit-juice–sweetened jam, put it on a plate, and carry it to the table with your grapefruit.

5. Go back to the kitchen, spoon the oatmeal into a bowl, and add some skim milk and a few raisins. Grab your tea cup and bowl, carry them back to the table, and sit down. Take a deep breath, smile, and look at your watch. It should now be about five minutes since you started. If you want to nuke your oatmeal in a microwave, you can follow the new-fangled directions on the old-fashioned oatmeal box, and have it ready in ninety seconds.

6. There are other ways to get your Victory Breakfast going while you're busy with morning activities. A friend of mine starts her oatmeal in a double boiler over medium heat. She then does a ten-minute exercise routine, showers, dresses, and then, about thirty minutes or so after starting, sits down to perfect oatmeal that she's not once had to stir or watch. She says it's hard to ruin oatmeal in a double boiler.

Now enjoy your breakfast. Especially if you've eaten a light dinner early the evening before, that oatmeal is going to taste heavenly. You'll relish the grapefruit and enjoy the toast. Eating at a comfortable pace, you can finish in five to seven minutes even if you're pressed for time (it's better to take ten minutes or so if you can).

So forget any excuse you might have that oatmeal takes too much time.

Okay, So You Really Can't Stand Oatmeal . . .

You've given oatmeal a fair shot, and it's driving you crazy. You've tried to eat the stuff every morning, but you can't quite pull it off—you've got to have a little variety! Don't panic—there's another Victory Breakfast that will give you many of the fiber and complex carbohydrate benefits of the oatmeal break-fast and that will allow you a little variety in your morning meal. Victory Breakfast #2 is built around the careful selection of healthy whole-grain cold cereals.

Trying to make a healthy selection from among the choices of ready-to-eat breakfast cereals is like tiptoeing through a minefield. Most have large amounts of salt, sugar, or fat, and most have had the fiber processed out. Some of them are even prepared with coconut or palm oil, two very popular ingredients in American processed food because they are cheap and they act as preservatives. They also happen to be two of the most highly saturated oils you can eat. Read the labels, because you absolutely must avoid any food with either of these two oils.

While none of the cereals on my Victory Breakfast #2 list can match the full benefits of the type of fiber contained in oatmeal, these cold cereals will still keep you regular, improve your health, and help you lose weight.

Here are three widely available breakfast cereals made of whole grains with very little (if any) added sugar, salt, or fat:

1. Nabisco Shredded Wheat n' Bran. Measuring total fiber and the lack of fat and added sugar and salt, this is the best cold cereal you can eat.

2. Nabisco Shredded Wheat. It doesn't have quite so much fiber as the version with added bran, but plain old Shredded Wheat is at the top of the list.

3. Kellogg's Nutri-Grain cereals. Although they have a little added salt, these fine cereals do retain the full fiber benefits of whole grains and don't have any added sugar or fat.

There are also two runner-ups: Post Grape Nuts has a little more salt than the others but is high in fiber and low in fat, Kellogg's All-Bran is very high in fiber but is also somewhat high in sugar and salt.

```
The Cold-Cereal Victory Breakfast


Half a Grapefruit

One large bowl of one of the following:
Shredded Wheat n' Bran,
Shredded Wheat,
or
Nutri-Grain
served with Skim Milk and, if desired,
Raisins

One slice Whole-Grain Toast
(Add a small amount of margarine if you wish)


1 cup Herbal Tea
or (if you must)
1 cup Coffee or Regular Tea
```

So you now have two Victory Breakfast menus to choose from. I still recommend eating the oatmeal breakfast as often as possible, but alternating with the cold-cereal breakfast when you feel you need a change.

What about the other ingredients in the two breakfast menus? They too are there to supply the added nutrients necessary for you to launch into your day at full speed.

Grapefruit

Generally speaking, I don't eat fruit with my meals (it agrees with some people and not with others). Grapefruit, though, is an exception if it is eaten before anything else or, preferably, even half an hour before eating the rest of breakfast. (If you don't have time in the mornings, don't worry.) Grapefruit clears your palate, and an average-sized grapefruit has very few calories. That's why it is so often found on "diet" breakfasts. A glass of *fresh* orange juice is okay, but it has more natural sugar than does grapefruit.

Milk

The 7-Week Victory Diet recommends that you eat oatmeal or cold cereal with *skim* milk. Even so-called low-fat milk is actually high in fat. Don't be misled by the "2 percent fat" on the label. That might not sound like much, but more than a third of the calories in a cup of 2 percent milk are from fat.

Type of milk (1 cup)	Total calories	Calories from fat	Percentage of fat calories
Whole (3.5% fat)	150	72	48
2% fat	120	42	35
Skim (0%)	86	4	5

This chart should make it clear why you need to drink skim milk. I know many of you will complain that it tastes watery. Once you get used to it, though, I guarantee that if you go back to whole milk it will taste sludgy and heavy.

Toast

A slice of whole-grain toast adds additional fiber and complex carbohydrates to your diet, and it is a good accompaniment to oatmeal. Make sure you eat toast made from the right bread. White bread is absolutely out. Be careful what kind of whole-grain bread you buy. Regular "brown" bread can be made from mostly enriched wheat flour (which isn't much better than enriched bleached white flour). Look for bread that lists as its first ingredient (the major one) whole-grain wheat flour. You'll then be assured of having the natural fiber of the whole grain. You may want to try one or two of the oat-bran breads currently on the market. New ones are coming out all the time, so be sure to check the ingredients.

Remember to go easy on margarine because it is pure fat, and gram for gram it has twice as many calories as the toast you put it on. Use margarine made with quality unsaturated oil—safflower oil is best.

Your Hot Beverage

Herbal tea is without doubt the best hot beverage you can drink in the morning. Regular tea isn't bad, and if you brew it for a minute or less, it has only about one fifth of the caffeine as a strong cup of coffee.

Starting your morning with coffee before you have anything else can be rough on your digestive system because the coffee acids hit your stomach lining before it is protected by any neutralizing foods. Whether the caffeine in coffee is bad for you is open to debate, although a recent Johns Hopkins University study showed that people who drank six or more cups a day had about 2½ times as many heart attacks as those who didn't (all other things being as equal as possible). If you drink only one cup a day, there is no evidence to show that it is specifically harmful.

Try to avoid caffeine, and especially coffee, if you can, but if you can't, try to substitute coffee with herbal tea, regular tea, or a coffee replacement such as Postum. In reading this book, you will learn that the diet profiles of famous and successful people show that most of them do not drink coffee; of the ones who do, each usually keeps it to one cup a day.

Hot Lemon Water: The Old-World Secret

People in traditional cultures always seem to establish, after a few generations of experimentation, a diet that takes best advantage of the food sources available to them. We can learn a lot of nutritional "secrets" by simply examining some of the eating habits of our grandparents and ancestors.

One such tradition—common in the "Old Country"—is the habit of drinking a glass of warm lemon water shortly after getting up in the morning. All you do is squeeze the juice of a single lemon into an eight-ounce glass of lukewarm water and drink it.

People in Eastern Europe have been doing this for generations. They've learned that warm lemon water is a wonderful cleansing agent. It soothes your throat and freshens your mouth, making your breakfast taste even better. One eight-ounce glass of warm lemon water is just what your body needs in the morning to rehydrate itself. The Vitamin C in the lemon has an enormous range of salubrious benefits. Drinking lemon water improves the health of your skin. That's why the warm lemon water habit is catching on quickly among actresses and fashion models such as Cheryl Tiegs.

There's no better way to start the day. If you want to, go ahead and add a half teaspoon of honey. It helps takes the edge off, but I've found I don't mind the tartness; in fact, I kind of enjoy puckering my lips.

 Winner's Circle Profile

Pat and Chris Riley

Chris Riley

In addition to her activities as mother and "coach's wife," Chris heads the Los Angeles Lakers Educational and Anti-Drug Program Charities.

Age: 39
Weight at 21: 118 pounds
Weight today: 118

BREAKFAST

One piece of dry whole-wheat toast, one orange or apple, and a bowl of oatmeal or cold cereal make up Chris' breakfast. Her son James (a preschooler) eats oatmeal almost every morning.

LUNCH

Chris eats tuna salad, celery, and one piece of whole-wheat toast with no margarine. Two or three times a week she has vegetable stew.

She also munches from what she calls her "button bag," a snack-mix of assorted sliced veggies.

DINNER

Most nights Chris eats green salad, chicken or fish, brown rice or potato, and vegetables. The Rileys alternate the fish or chicken with pasta. Chris always eats between 6:00 and 7:30 P.M.

EXERCISE

Chris rides a stationary bike for 30 minutes, three to four times a week. She also follows a low-volume program of light weight lifting for upper body development.

COMMENTS

Chris takes her "rabbit food" (her button bag) whenever she leaves the house. The bag includes fresh carrots, peppers, broccoli, cauliflower, and other assorted cleaned and sliced fresh veggies. She nibbles from her button bag through the day, steering clear of less nutritious snacks, and filling in if she has to eat a hurried lunch.

Chris feels that no one eats better than her young son; she can remember visiting McDonald's only twice. She does like occasional desserts, as does Pat, but she tries to keep them to a minimum.

(continued)

Pat Riley

Pat is Head Coach of the World Champion Los Angeles Lakers.

Age: 42
Weight at 21: 215 pounds
Weight today: 205 pounds

BREAKFAST

When at home and not on the road, Pat has two cups of decaffeinated coffee, whole-wheat buttered toast with sliced tomatoes, a large orange juice, and oatmeal or whole-grain cereal.

LUNCH

Every day Pat has one tuna or turkey sandwich on whole-wheat bread or toast with iced tea—no sweetener or sugar.

DINNER

Pat eats the same dinner as Chris.

EXERCISE

Pat completes a daily short workout with weights. During a game he will unconsciously do at least fifty full squats.

COMMENTS

Professional coaching, especially football and basketball, is probably one of the more stress-

producing, gut-wrenching, demanding profes-
sions.

If you want to look at intensity, turn on your
television and watch any NBA or NFL football
coach during a game, and observe the tense-
ness in their faces. Pat is no exception. After
winning two World Championships back to
back, he knows the value of eating properly
and staying in shape, not just for himself but
for his family and players. Pat is an extremely
success-oriented individual, and it shows in his
own personal health and fitness. Once in a
while, after a particularly satisfying win, Pat
has been known to indulge in a piece of chocolate cake. Since the Lakers win a lot, however, he keeps the cake to a minimum.

◄ ◄ 5 ► ►

Eat Breakfast like a King—*Why* You Need to Eat It

Chapter 4 discussed *what* you should be eating for breakfast each day. This chapter explains *why* you need to eat a big breakfast that is selected from only two simple menus and *why* those menus need to be based around low-fat, whole-grain oats and cereal.

Complex Carbohydrates: What the Rest of the World Has Been Eating for 10,000 Years

So-called primitive peoples around the world always seem to figure out the best diet for the food sources available to them. If only we in our modern civilizations could do as well!

Take the famous Sherpa people, for example, who live in the vicinity of Mount Everest in the Himalayas. They eat a diet composed primarily of potatoes and barley. Rick Ridgeway, who helped write this book, is a mountain climber who has twice been to Everest; on both expeditions he and his team had Sherpas help them backpack their loads of equipment and food up the mountain. These hardy people would get up early in the mornings and prepare for their daily load-carrying by eating a huge breakfast of either a barley flour dough called *tsampa,* or boiled potatoes—a dozen or more potatoes per person—washed down with a little tea spiked with yak milk. They would then shoulder backpacks loaded with thirty-five to forty pounds of gear and set off for the upper camp, climbing 4,000 vertical feet up an immense ice face to an altitude of 26,000 feet without benefit of supplemental oxygen.

They would then cache their loads and return, sliding quickly down the ice face using the ropes fixed in place, and be back in camp in time for lunch. And what did they eat? You guessed it: more potatoes (and not hashed brown potatoes, either, but low-fat, high-energy, steamed or roasted potatoes).

The same emphasis on complex carbohydrates can be found by studying the eating habits of most cultures since the time we humans became an agricultural species more than 10,000 years ago. If you look around the world today at the diets of most of the people on this earth—especially rural Asians and Africans, the ones who don't suffer the convenience of fast foods (although there may not be many left)—you will find that complex carbohydrates make up 70 percent or more of their caloric intake.

What about our culture? What about the Standard American Diet? Well, it truly is S.A.D., because complex carbohydrates currently make up only about 22 percent of the total calories that the average American eats. The percentage wasn't always so low, though. At the turn of the century, before the current onslaught of processed foods, the percentage of complex carbohydrates in the average American's diet was up around 45 percent.

Today, there is a strong consensus among qualified nutritionists that 50 to 70 percent of our daily caloric intake should be carbohydrates and that most of that should be from complex carbohydrates.

But just what are complex carbohydrates?

Chemically speaking, complex carbohydrates are long chains of simple sugars linked together. They are found in starchy foods such as bread and cereal, grains (including rice and barley), vegetables (including potatoes, carrots, and broccoli), beans, and fruit. Practically speaking, there are only two points you really need to know about complex carbohydrates:

1. After you eat complex carbohydrates, they break down into glucose—just as simple sugar does—but at a much slower rate so as not to trigger the release of insulin. This is important because eating complex carbohydrates gives you long-lasting energy without significantly altering your blood sugar level.

2. Complex carbohydrates are not fattening. Gram for gram they have the same number of calories as protein and only half as many calories as oils and animal fat. Because they burn slowly, your body tends to convert complex carbohydrates into energy instead of into fat.

And energy is just what you need most of the morning. That's why breakfast is the perfect time of day to load up on complex carbohydrates. You need the high energy of fuel-rich complex carbohydrates to boost you into your active cycle.

I don't suggest that you need to eat fifteen potatoes each morning, stocking up on carbohydrates as the Sherpas do—unless that's in keeping with your tastes and preferences. But you can get the same high-energy boost by eating a big whole-grain breakfast. In other words, you need the Oatmeal or Whole-Grain Cold-Cereal Victory Breakfast.

But why do I recommend that you eat breakfast from only

two basic menus? And why do I also recommend that you eat a big breakfast—a bowl and a half of cereal, or even more if you are still hungry? Let's take a look.

Why You Should Eat the Same Kind of Breakfast Every Day

If you are like most people, you already *are* eating the same kind of breakfast every morning.

If you don't believe me, think about what you've had for breakfast each day this last week. There's a very good chance that you'll realize you belong with the majority of Americans who eat nearly the same thing every morning.

How do I know this is true? Remember that survey that was taken on a typical weekend in the Phoenix shopping center? Here are a few of the questions from that survey that pertained to breakfast:

1. What do you usually eat for breakfast?

Cereal (hot or cold)	32%
Toast only	27%
Bacon and eggs	21%
Nothing	20%

2. Do you eat basically the same breakfast at least five days a week?

Yes	73%
No	27%

3. How many cups of coffee do you drink in the morning?

One	28%
Two	22%
Three or more	16%
None	34%

The survey showed that 73 percent—a very strong major-ity—ate the same food for breakfast at least five days a week. And that is why I am confident that you will have no problem converting to the Victory Breakfast. All you have to do is substitute one breakfast for another.

But why eat the same breakfast every day? There are three big reasons.

1. It's easy. In contrast to every other diet plan I've ever read, *The 7-Week Victory Diet* has no complicated recipes to follow. You don't have to buy exotic fruits, prepare special grain pancakes, mix egg substitutes, or search the grocery aisles for low-calorie syrup. You don't have to follow any complex menu plans that have you eating different things each morning of the week. I know that as a busy person you probably don't have time to shop, cook, and eat complex meals, especially for breakfast. And if you already eat the same thing for breakfast most days of the week, why change a comfortable habit—especially when you can pre-pare and eat the Victory Breakfast in only ten minutes!

2. It's habit forming. You'll find that once you get in the habit of eating the Victory Breakfast every morning, you'll look forward to it. You'll be hooked, and it will be easy to resist any tendency to eat a breakfast laden with saturated fats, or to skip breakfast—a mistake just as harmful as eating a fattening breakfast.

But don't take my word for it. Look through this book and examine the breakfast-eating habits of the prominent and successful people whom I profile in the Winner's Circle. You'll find that all of them eat big breakfasts, all of them eat the same kind of breakfast, and nearly all of them say breakfast is their favorite meal of the day!

3. It will help you lose weight. As I'll explain in a minute, both of my breakfast menus are low in calories and high in the nutrients and fiber that help you stay lean and healthy.

Those are the reasons to get in the habit of eating the same oatmeal or whole-grain Victory Breakfast every day. Now let's look at the reason why you also want to get in the habit of eating a big breakfast.

Why a Big Breakfast Helps You Lose Weight

I've already explained that eating breakfast is important because it gives you the energy to switch from your rest cycle to your active cycle.

But you want not only to eat breakfast but also to eat a big breakfast. You should eat one-and-one-half servings of either oatmeal or a select whole-grain cold cereal. Then, if you are still hungry, eat another bowl. *It will not make you fat,* and here's why:

1. A big breakfast of oatmeal or whole-grain cereal gives you the energy you need to launch your day, and it patterns the rest of your day's meals and snacks. Studies at Rockefeller University have shown that eating a light breakfast or skipping breakfast altogether throws your brain's neurotransmitters out of balance. These are the chemicals that control hunger, and—when they are in proper balance—keep you from going on food binges.

    By eating a big breakfast—by keeping your metabolism in balance—you will avoid the midmorning doughnut-and-coffee break. This in turn will set you up to eat a Victory Lunch, and that in turn will set you up to eat a Victory Dinner. And eating a Victory Dinner, in turn, sets you up to wake the next day alert and hungry, ready again to enjoy a healthy breakfast. If you eat a Victory Dinner and then have nothing before bed but fruit or cereal, I guarantee that you'll wake up looking forward to enjoying another oatmeal breakfast.

2. A big breakfast of oatmeal or whole-grain cereal gives you a high intake of dietary fiber, which helps you quickly pass wastes through your system. *This is extremely important both for your weight control and for your health.* When your food flushes through your system in twenty-four hours or less, there is little time for food to linger in your system where it can be converted to fat. A high-fiber diet helps you lose weight. Furthermore, scientists now suggest that getting food quickly through your system prevents any toxic substances you may ingest from lingering against the walls and lining of your digestive system, encouraging the development of diseases such as diverticulosis and colon cancer.

Diverticulosis and its cousin diverticulitis are two problems of the lower intestine caused by fiber-poor diets. Their symptoms are gas pains, heartburn, nausea, cramping, and constipation, and they afflict a huge segment of our population. In fact, 50 percent of Americans over fifty years of age suffer diverticulosis—and nearly all the cases are caused by insufficient fiber in the diet. That fact alone is reason enough to adopt oatmeal as your breakfast of choice!

What Is Fiber and How Does It Work?

People are sometimes surprised to learn that fiber is also a complex carbohydrate, but a type that is chemically so tough that it won't break down in your stomach or intestines. The fact that fiber cannot be digested is the very reason it's a valuable aid to your digestion.

The way fiber works is simple. After you eat foods rich in fiber, the chemicals in your digestive system start to break down the food so it can pass into your system. Fiber resists this chemical action, and because it remains in its original state, it adds bulk to the rest of the food you *are* digesting. This bulk allows that food to pass more easily through your stomach and intestines, benefiting your entire system in a number of ways:

1. Quick and frequent passage of wastes cleans your system, allowing carcinogens less chance to linger in contact with your intestinal walls. Studies have shown that a high-fiber diet cleans out your intestines and reduces your risk of colon cancer.

2. A diet high in soluble fiber—the kind of fiber found in oatmeal—may help lower your serum cholesterol. While scientists aren't certain exactly how this works, they do know that eating foods, like oatmeal, that are high in soluble fiber cleans bile from your system that otherwise would linger and act as an agent in the manufacture of more cholesterol.

   Wheat, on the other hand, contains mostly insoluble fiber, which still aids digestion and cleans your intestines, but doesn't appear to be as effective as oatmeal in lowering your cholesterol. That's why I recommend you eat the Victory Oatmeal Breakfast as often as possible, substituting the Victory Cold-Cereal Breakfast only when you need an occasional change.

3. A high-fiber diet—whether soluble or insoluble—takes the strain out of your morning bowel movement, which in turn reduces your risk of diverticulosis later in life.

   I mentioned earlier that 50 percent of Americans over age fifty suffer from problems of the lower intestine. I find this statistic almost mind-boggling. Imagine a painful disease that afflicts the majority of Americans over age fifty and that hardly anyone talks about. How can this be? Why isn't there more press on this subject?

   The reason, I believe, is rooted in the shyness most Americans feel when trying to talk frankly about regularity and bowel movements. If you think about it, being afraid to talk about this subject is downright silly, especially considering the dire consequences of not understanding the importance of regular, healthy bowel movements. I think it's time for a little unabashed discussion.

Diverticulosis: The Disease of the '90s

Diverticulosis and diverticulitis are the most common diseases of the colon. Diverticulosis is a weakening of the lower intestine caused by years of trying to pass hard stools. This continued straining creates weak points in the colon wall that then bulge out into little sacs. This affects digestion and leads to a host of painful and irritating problems such as gas, cramps, constipation, nausea, heartburn, and rectal tenderness.

If any of these pouches or weak points in the colon become infected—and this happens at one time or another to 20 percent of those with this problem—the result is diverticulitis, an even more painful problem that can have very serious consequences, including death.

Both diverticulosis and diverticulitis are directly related to lack of fiber in the diet. In fact, these two diseases were almost unheard of until the 1920s. As the popularity of processed, instant, and junk foods began to grow, however, so did the incidence of diverticulosis. I can't think of a more glaring condemnation of the American food industry and the Standard American Diet than this single fact.

Diverticulosis can sometimes take forty years to develop— forty years of bad eating habits. That's why it's so important to begin eating a high-fiber, complex carbohydrate diet—NOW!

How can you tell if you have enough fiber in your diet? How do you know if you are putting unusual strains on your lower digestive tract?

The answer is simple: Look at your stool. Let's face it, most people do this anyway, so there's no harm in being frank: What you want every morning is a big stool. The bigger the better. What you want is a daily bowel movement that is soft, easy to pass, and, if your diet is correct, does not smell foul. What you do not want is a bowel movement every other day made up of small, hard pellets that you strain to pass. You want one big floater, not a dozen little sinkers.

If you adopt an oatmeal or whole-grain breakfast, you will manufacture very big floaters. If you've never eaten a high-fiber diet, you won't believe the difference this can make. You won't believe that up until now you've been harboring all that waste in your system. A big dumbrowski in the morning means that your food is passing through your system in twenty-four hours or less. It means any carcinogenic chemicals are lingering for less time against your intestines, and it means less strain is being put on your intestinal walls.

When you start passing high-fiber, high-bulk stools, you'll quickly discover you feel healthier and cleaner. Then you'll notice that you start to lose weight. And the more whole grains you eat for breakfast—especially oatmeal—the more weight you'll lose.

Now if that isn't enough, remember that eating fiber-rich foods can also help you to control your weight because fiber fills you up. Eating high-fiber foods leaves you satisfied, nutritionally fulfilled, and slim.

One final note. Because some fiber is absorbent—especially the fiber in oatmeal—it's important to drink plenty of water so that the fiber can achieve its bulk and do your system the most good. Five to six glasses of water a day, in addition to any other liquids taken in, is the recommended amount for optimum benefit.

Eating foods high in fiber is addicting. You can prove this to yourself in a simple experiment that should remove any doubts you may have about fiber's benefits. Go on the Victory Breakfast plan for three weeks. Then go back to your old low-fiber eating habits for a couple of days. The first thing you'll notice is that you become constipated. Then you'll get a head-ache and feel sluggish because of all the wastes that are once again accumulating in your system. I guarantee that you'll want to go back to your high-fiber Victory Breakfast right away, and you won't want to go off of it again.

You *Can* Eat All You Want for Breakfast

You may be one of those people who has no appetite for breakfast. You wake up, and all you want is to shower, get dressed, and grab a cup of coffee as you head out the door. Breakfast is the last thing on your mind.

If you are one of those people, I'll bet you the reason you're not hungry in the morning is because you ate dinner late and you ate dinner big. If you didn't eat big, you probably had a good-sized snack before going to bed—maybe a bowl of chocolate chip ice cream.

I guarantee that if you follow the Victory Breakfast, Lunch, Dinner, and Snack Diet, you'll wake up famished, ready to set the correct pattern for your day's eating by starting with a big breakfast.

If you think eating a large bowl of oatmeal will make you fat, you're wrong again. First, consider this chart:

The Oatmeal Victory Breakfast

One large serving of cooked oatmeal	123 calories
1 cup skim milk	88 calories
1 slice whole-wheat toast	66 calories
1 pat margarine	36 calories
Half a grapefruit	40 calories
Lemon water	20 calories
1 cup tea	0 calories
Total	373 calories

And if you are still hungry, you can eat another bowl of oatmeal and still be under 500 calories!

Compare that to the standard bacon-and-egg or sausage-and-egg breakfast, complete with a serving of hash browns. Depending on the fat content of the meat and on how much butter and oil are used in cooking, this breakfast will total anywhere between 800 and 2,000 calories.

The Victory Breakfast Sets You Up for the Victory Lunch

Each meal you eat has an effect on the next meal you eat. If you have coffee and a piece of toast for breakfast, you'll feel famished way before lunch, and by midmorning you'll give in to the coffee-and-doughnut wagon. If you eat a big, nourishing breakfast, you'll not only have energy to carry you through the morning—energy that will allow you to think clearly and to work hard—but also you'll arrive at your midday meal without feeling as if you have to devour everything in sight as quickly as possible. You'll be set up to eat the Victory Lunch, the subject of the next chapter.

Jack Valenti

In addition to his work as author and lecturer, Jack is president of the Motion Picture Association of America. He was formerly special assistant to Lyndon Johnson.

Age: 65
Weight at 21:   145 pounds
Weight today: 148 pounds

BREAKFAST

Each morning of the week (including Sunday) Jack has half a grapefruit or fresh orange juice plus Nutri-Grain cereal with skim milk. He does not drink coffee.

LUNCH

Every day Jack has either a tuna salad or fruit salad.

DINNER

Jack's wife, Mary Margaret, is an excellent cook, and Jack likes to eat a substantial dinner. Nevertheless, on most evenings he eats from only a few basic recipes. Favorites include pasta (two nights a week), and fish or poultry (two nights a week.) On weekends Jack occasionally cuts loose and has a hamburger. He never eats dessert. He has an occasional beer or two.

EXERCISE

Three days a week Jack tries to get a complete workout that includes stomach exercises and stretching. On alternate days he does fifteen minutes of stretching in the morning, and on weekends he plays strong singles tennis.

Jack has one diet ritual he performs every morning at the same time: He gets on his bathroom scale and checks his weight. If he's over his target weight, he eats lightly until he's back to 148 pounds. Jack has a murderous travel schedule, but in all the years I've known him he never wavers from his menu or exercise routine, whether he's traveling or not.

◄ ◄ **6** ► ►

Eat Lunch like a Prince

Have you ever wondered why many Latin Americans are overweight? One reason is because most of them have only *cafe con leche* and a sugar pastry for breakfast.

Have you ever stopped to think why so many Latin Americans take a siesta in the afternoon? After that paltry breakfast they're starved, so they gorge themselves on a large lunch.

Consider the midday meal of a typical middle-class family in Peru. They start with soup, often something like meatballs in a heavy cream-based broth. Then comes the main course, usually a meat dish. Favorites include breaded and pan-fried steak, stewed chicken, or guinea pig with a thick chili sauce (guinea pig is a traditional Peruvian dish, a little like rabbit). There are large servings of rice, potatoes, and yucca, a local tuber. A big basket of white bread next to a butter dish is a permanent fixture, and after everything comes dessert, often something like custard with caramel syrup ladled over it.

After that, they don't *have* any choice but to take a siesta.

There was a time when I too suffered the urge to take an afternoon siesta. I had the problem during high school, and I bet there's a good chance you had it, too. Remember your 1:00 P.M. class? Maybe you don't, because if you were like me you were always sleeping. Why? Because we got up in the morning, grabbed a doughnut and a glass of milk, dashed off to school, were famished by lunch, and proceeded to down a hot dog or bologna sandwich on white bread, potato chips, plus a Coke or a milk shake from the school snack bar.

Our bodies had to work hard to digest all this stuff, so our blood rushed from our heads to our stomachs to accomplish this formidable task, and—surprise!—we fell asleep in the after-lunch class.

What we should have been doing was eating a Victory Breakfast. If we had been in the oatmeal habit every morning of every school day, it would have been easy to eat a Victory Lunch. Then there would have been no problem staying awake during the 1:00 P.M. class.

The thing is, a 1:00 P.M. class is no different from a 1:00 P.M. business meeting. In either situation, you need to eat right to stay alert. Here's how you can do it.

How Simple It Is!

The 7-Week Victory Diet is based on simplicity. It advocates using only a few basic recipes—a few basic Victory Recipes—because you already eat from only a few basic recipes anyway.

You've seen how easy it is to eat nearly the same thing for breakfast every morning. To a great extent the same is true for lunch. You *can* get in the habit of eating the same kind of lunch most days, although the Victory Diet does allow you to add more variety than at breakfast. With lunch, for example, it may be impossible for you to eat the same thing every day, especially if, because of business, you often eat in restaurants.

Even if you do eat frequently in restaurants, you can still stay with the Victory Lunch by choosing those dishes on the restaurant menu that are closest to the Victory Lunch menus.

The "Lunch like a Prince" Strategy

If you eat a big Victory Breakfast, you won't be tempted by that midmorning coffee break when so many people fall into the Danish, doughnut, or cookie trap.

You *will* be ready for something to eat by lunchtime, however, and that's when you want to eat a medium-sized meal. Size is important—you don't want the meal to be so big that it puts you to sleep, but you don't want it to be so small that you are famished by dinnertime, either.

The quantity you eat is important, as is the content of your lunch. The strategy for what I've included in the Victory Lunch menus is simple. As with the breakfast menus, the lunch menus are low in fat. But unlike breakfast, the lunch menus are high in protein.

Protein—Eat a Little, and Eat It at Lunch

Most of us grew up believing we had to eat protein if we expected to be strong. We also grew up believing that high-protein diets were a good way to lose weight. Steak leads to strength; high protein leads to trim, hard bodies.

Most nutritionists now realize that those beliefs are not accurate. Preindustrial agricultural peoples didn't subsist on high-protein diets—they relied on complex carbohydrates. Similarly, we don't need a lot of protein in our own diets, either. The RDA (Recommended Dietary Allowance, set by a committee from the National Academy of Sciences) for protein is 56 grams per day for adult men and 44 grams for adult women. How much is that?

How much protein does the average American eat? A survey of several thousand men and women made in the early 1970s showed men ate an average of 102 grams of protein a day, and women 70 grams a day. That's almost twice the RDA.

Why should you eat a lunch high in protein, then? To answer that, let's take a look at what protein is.

Protein is one of the three major food categories (carbohydrates and fats are the other two), and it is a primary source of amino acids. In fact, amino acids are what protein is made of. There are more then twenty types of amino acids, and all but eight of them can be manufactured by our bodies. These eight, however, are essential to continued good health—they are, in fact, called the essential amino acids—and they have to be acquired through the food we eat.

It is important, therefore, that you include protein in your diet, but most knowledgeable nutritionists agree that protein shouldn't contribute more than 15 to 20 percent of the total calories you consume.

Red meat, chicken, and fish contain all the amino acids, including the eight essential amino acids, in a balance ideally suited to human needs. Plant foods also contain amino acids but not in the same balance as meat products. By eating plant foods in the right combination, however (e.g., grains with beans), it's possible to obtain the full complement of amino acids and to fulfill the body's protein requirements. Red meat is an ideal source of protein, but the danger of getting your protein from red meat is that it comes packaged with more fat than does chicken or fish. You might get all the protein you need (and then some) from a small piece of steak, but you'll also be getting a lot of fat high in saturated oil and cholesterol.

That's why the Victory Lunch menus revolve around meals featuring fish and chicken.

But why eat the protein you need at lunch?

Because research has shown that eating protein releases an amino acid called tyrosine, which stimulates mental alertness. In other words, to achieve maximum mental alertness after you eat, you want a medium-portion, high-protein meal. Because early afternoon is the time of day when most of us are feeling sluggish, it makes sense to eat most of our daily protein quota at lunch.

Here then are the four Victory Lunches, starting with my favorite, the lunch I eat four or five days a week:

Victory Lunch #1

The Thin-Win Lunch

Tuna Salad
(Delicious water-packed albacore tuna made with low-oil mayonnaise and served on a bed of crisp lettuce)

Ak-Mak Crackers
(A few crisp, low-salt, whole-grain Armenian-style crackers)

Celery Sticks

Cranberry Juice Cocktail
(A thirst-quenching 50/50 mixture of cranberry juice and mineral water or Perrier)
or
Iced Tea

Let's look more closely at this meal plan. The first thing to notice is that it's not too big. You want to make certain you eat enough to feel satisfied and that you eat enough to get you through comfortably to dinnertime. You don't want to eat so much that your body goes into overtime working to digest it, and you go into a slumber for the next hour or two.

If you've eaten a Victory Breakfast earlier in the day, this sized lunch should suit you perfectly. Vary the portions a little according to your size. Again, make certain you eat enough to feel satisfied.

Now let's look at the ingredients, starting with the tuna salad. There are five reasons to choose tuna for your midday fare.

1. It tastes good, and that's paramount if you're going to eat it every day.

2. It's easy to prepare. Try mixing up a two- or three-day supply and store it in the fridge. It's easy to brown-bag a tuna-salad lunch to work. You can also make a tuna sandwich on whole-wheat bread if you like.

3. Tuna is an oily fish, and evidence is growing that fish oil is an agent that actually helps lower serum cholesterol because it increases the amount of high-density lipoprotein (HDL) in your blood. HDL is a chemical that binds cholesterol and prevents it from adhering to your arterial walls.

4. Fish is very high in protein (and we've seen why it's a good idea to eat most of the protein you'll consume in a given day with your noontime meal).

5. You can usually find tuna salad or individual cans of tuna (no mayonnaise) on restaurant lunch menus. By getting in the habit of eating tuna salad for lunch most days, you can easily get into the habit of eating healthy lunches when you're in a restaurant.

Tuna contains hardly any saturated fat so long as you buy the water-packed variety, and you don't mix in too much mayonnaise, which is almost pure oil and fat. Keep mayonnaise down to one tablespoon per lunch-serving, or try substituting yogurt or low-calorie mayonnaise. (One tablespoon of regular mayonnaise has as many calories as an average-sized baked potato!) Another solution is to make your own mayonnaise substitute. I've found the recipes in Haas's *Eat to Win* and Jane Brody's *Good Food Book* to be winners.

The other ingredients in my lunch are chosen to complement the tuna salad. Celery is one of the most nutritious vegetables you can eat, full of vitamins, minerals, and lots of fiber. (It's also the one food that takes more calories to eat and digest than it contains.) You can substitute other vegetables, though, if you want occasional variety. Try carrot sticks, red pepper, snow peas, or jicama.

Crackers are tough: It's hard to find good ones. I like Ak-Mak because they are made with whole grain, they are low in salt and saturated fat, and they taste delicious. If your grocer doesn't stock them, here are a few additional crackers you can substitute:

- Whole-Wheat Matzo (these crackers are made of whole wheat, with no fat and very little salt)

- Finn Crisp

- Devonshire Wheat Melba Toast

- Zweiback

Cranberry juice deserves special mention. First, the reason I cut it with mineral water or soda is to reduce the fructose (sugar) content of the drink and to make it taste better. To me, straight cranberry juice is just too sweet. Cranapple is slightly less sweet, so it's a good choice, too (I also like fresh apple juice cut 50/50 by mineral water).

Cranberry juice, even diluted, has some health benefits,

and this is one area of nutrition many doctors seem to have caught on to. It's common to prescribe cranberry juice to patients with urinary tract infections and prostate problems. Cranberry juice is also a strong prophylactic against these problems, so I recommend it as a midday drink three or four days a week. You should drink only one glass, though, because too much liquid with a meal can impede digestion by diluting the digestive juices and acids that must work to break down your food.

Victory Lunch #2

The Victory Lunch #2 is a favorite that comes from a little planning. When you cook chicken for dinner, add a couple of extra legs and have them for lunch the next day or two. By adding an extra breast, you can have chicken salad instead of tuna salad. Be certain to remove the skin *before* cooking.

Chicken Italiano

Cold Chicken Leg or Breast and
Sliced Tomatoes with a thin slice of
Mozzarella Cheese
(*Optional: fresh basil leaves between the tomato and cheese*)

Rye Toast with Safflower Margarine

Cranberry Juice Cocktail
(*A thirst-quenching 50/50 mixture of cranberry juice and mineral water or Perrier*)
or
Iced Tea

Victory Lunch #3

The Victory Lunch #3 is easy if you are eating lunch at home. It helps to have leftovers from your previous day's dinner.

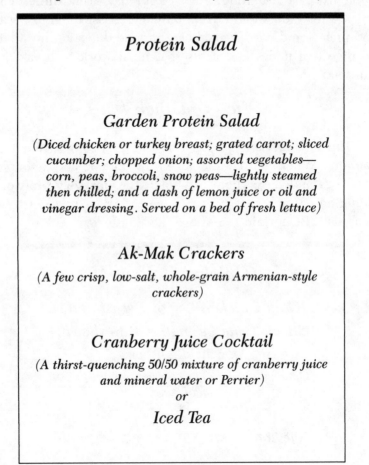

Protein Salad

Garden Protein Salad

(Diced chicken or turkey breast; grated carrot; sliced cucumber; chopped onion; assorted vegetables— corn, peas, broccoli, snow peas—lightly steamed then chilled; and a dash of lemon juice or oil and vinegar dressing. Served on a bed of fresh lettuce)

Ak-Mak Crackers

(A few crisp, low-salt, whole-grain Armenian-style crackers)

Cranberry Juice Cocktail

(A thirst-quenching 50/50 mixture of cranberry juice and mineral water or Perrier)
or

Iced Tea

Victory Lunch #4

The Victory Lunch #4 is simple, low in salt, low in cholesterol, and has a terrific protein punch.

Seafood Delight

Shrimp or Crab Salad

(Shrimp or shredded crabmeat served on a bed of leafy green lettuce with a dash of lemon juice, one tablespoon of mayonnaise, or oil and vinegar dressing, or curry sauce)

Celery Sticks

Ak-Mak Crackers

(A few crisp, low-salt, whole-grain Armenian-style crackers)

Cranberry Juice Cocktail

(A thirst-quenching 50/50 mixture of cranberry juice and mineral water or Perrier)

or

Iced Tea or Hot Herbal Tea

The Bigger the Deal You Have to Make, the Lighter the Lunch You Need to Eat

"Let's discuss it over lunch" is a business phrase that has gotten a lot of people in trouble. One of my ground rules in my own business is *Never discuss anything important over lunch*. You just are not as sharp when you're eating. Eating distracts from clear thinking simply because having food in your stomach diminishes your mental acuity.

If I'm put in a situation where I have no choice (as many of you are) but to attend a lunch where I know important business is going to be discussed, I try to eat a fruit snack late in the morning. Then when the time comes, I order a very small lunch. That way I can concentrate on the business at hand instead of concentrating on jamming food into my mouth while trying to make a deal at the same time.

There's an additional corollary to my strategy that you may already have realized: My small lunch also leaves me one-up over whomever I'm dealing with, especially if they're big-lunch eaters. And if they're the beer, wine, or martini-for-lunch type, then I may be faced with the dilemma of making a moral decision whether or not to take advantage of someone who is essentially a handicapped person.

Don't Work at Lunch—Enjoy It

For some of the same reasons, you shouldn't make deals over lunch; nor should you try to do other work over lunch. Make your lunchtime your breaktime. It's better for your digestion, and by taking a break you're likely to get more work done in the long run anyway.

Another tip is to eat lunch outside, in the sunshine, as much as possible. It's a habit that a lot of people in New York follow, weather permitting. Walk down almost any avenue at lunchtime, and you'll see hundreds of people sitting outside on the steps, taking a break. It will do your spirit good to trade fluorescent light for sunlight, and it will do your health good: You need sunlight each day for your body to synthesize Vitamin D, which is essential to your ability to absorb calcium and phosphorus.

As with breakfast, what you eat for lunch affects what you eat for the meal that follows. It's all interconnected, and eating the Victory Lunch is the only way you'll be in position to eat the Victory Dinner.

Janet Leigh

Janet is best known for her acting career. She is also a successful author and an avid skier, which helps keep her looking as good today as she did at MGM years ago.

Age: 60
Weight at 21: 114 pounds
Weight today: 105 pounds

BREAKFAST

She begins with juice or fruit, and continues with one piece of toast with low-fat margarine; and whole-grain cereal with skim milk, alternating Shredded Wheat with oatmeal. She occasionally has a bagel and cream cheese on the weekends, but never has coffee or tea.

LUNCH

Janet alternates between a tuna sandwich on whole-wheat bread and a cup of soup with a green salad.

DINNER

Pasta or chicken or fish; vegetables; and, about once a week, a piece of ground, lean sirloin provide the dinner menu, which is usually complemented with one glass of wine or beer.

EXERCISE

Janet's exercise is doubles tennis twice a week, treadmill twice a week for twenty minutes, and "running around the town all day, every day."

COMMENTS

Janet is co-founder and past president of SHARE, the preeminent Los Angeles charity that benefits retarded children. SHARE has raised many millions of dollars during the past thirty years.

Janet has been married to Bob Brandt for twenty-five years. A securities broker, Bob leaves for the office every morning at 5:00 A.M., so Janet has to adjust her schedule, especially her meal schedule, to conform with Bob's. They usually eat dinner early and go to bed early.

Eat Dinner like a Pauper

Eating dinner like a pauper doesn't mean you should eat poorly; it means you should eat properly. If you're like most people, dinner is the social focus of your day, the time when you get together with loved ones and share your day's experiences. It's also the time when you feel as if you need that extra beer or glass of wine, that you've earned that bowl of chocolate–chocolate-chip ice cream for dessert.

That doesn't mean it's impossible, or even difficult, to learn good dinner habits. You won't find it very hard, for example, to eat a medium-sized or even small-sized dinner if you've eaten a big breakfast, a medium-sized lunch, and have had an afternoon snack.

What you eat for one meal influences what you eat in the next meal. But that's not the only factor. *When* you eat your meals also is a big ingredient in setting your daily eating pattern.

That's why one of the most important rules of *The 7-Week Victory Diet* is:

Eat dinner no later than three hours before going to bed.

There are two big reasons you should eat dinner early:

1. Eating dinner early means you have time to burn off some of your meal before going to sleep. This helps keep you slim and helps you sleep better.
2. Eating dinner early means you'll wake up hungry, ready to set your day's eating patterns with a big breakfast.

But why three hours before going to sleep? Since there's a good chance you sleep between seven and eight hours a night, eating dinner three hours before going to bed means you'll wake up the next morning hungry and ready for a big breakfast. If you go to bed at 10:30, for example, then following my recommendations you will have finished dinner at 7:30. You'll probably get up the next morning around 6:30, and have breakfast about 7:00. That means it will have been nearly twelve hours since you had dinner, and I guarantee that you'll be ready for a big breakfast. You'll be ready to set the right eating pattern for the rest of your day.

I know many of you may resist the idea of eating dinner early. It's natural to resist new ideas and to resist changing habits. But if you really want to lose weight and have a healthier body, then you've got to be able to change. Successful people such as the ones profiled in this book, people who take charge of their lives so they can get slim, trim, and healthy, are people who look at a new idea without prejudice. If the new idea makes sense, they try it. Successful people don't ask why, *they ask why not*.

How to Eat Dinner Early if You Have to Work Late

So you've got to work late. There's a report due the next day, you've got to finish an important presentation, or whatever. Normally you'd get home by 7:00, follow the Victory Plan and eat dinner by 8:00, go to bed at 11:00. But tonight you won't even be home by 11:00.

The solution? Take your dinner to work, and eat it on schedule. Take an extra sack "lunch," if necessary, and have it for dinner. Take plenty of fruit for snacks between your meals, too. That way you won't interrupt your usual eating pattern, and even though you may have to interrupt your usual sleeping pattern, the effect won't be as debilitating because at least your mealtimes will remain on schedule. Plus you'll find that the food gives you an energy boost to keep your mental gears going.

Eat from Simple Menus

To make it easier to get in the habit of eating dinner early, it's important to eat a simple dinner. The reason: When you eat early you often have less time to prepare dinner, so it's all the more important to have a few easy recipes from which to choose.

To lose weight permanently in an easy-to-follow plan, you need only eat from my five basic dinner menus. Again, I know some of you will think this is restrictive, that you can't eat only five different dinner meals. But hold on! If you are like most Americans, remember that you usually eat from only a few favorite recipes anyway. Chances are you already have about a half-dozen dinners that you prepare most evenings. So all I'm asking is that you replace the meals you are now eating with the menus from the Victory Diet.

And once you get in the comfortable habit of eating the

Victory Dinner menus, you'll look forward to them each evening. Remember, too, that once you reach your target weight you can design your own favorite repertoire of a half-dozen dinners that fit within the Victory Diet guidelines.

But I bet that when you reach your target weight, you'll be so used to enjoying the five dinner menus I recommend that you'll keep most of them as your own favorite dinners.

The Five Dinner Menus of the 7-Week Victory Diet

Victory Dinner #1

Pasta Plus

(Thin noodles cooked al dente with a bit of melted margarine and a few fresh garlic cloves, and topped with a dash of Parmesan cheese)

Tossed Salad

(Oil and vinegar dressing)

Steamed Broccoli

Glass of Wine

You can eat the Victory Dinner #1 up to four times a week; I do. The only qualification I would make to is to skip the wine if you're overweight.

Now let's take a closer look at the individual ingredients.

Pasta

Contrary to popular belief, pasta is not fattening. By itself, it is only starch, the complex carbohydrate that should be the staple of everyone's diet. The only thing lacking from most pasta is fiber, and that's why I like whole-wheat pasta best. Pasta has a reputation as being fattening because of the fat-laden sauces with which it is often served.

The garlic margarine sauce I enjoy on pasta is reasonably low in calories and, equally important, it is low in saturated fats. Feel free to vary the sauce you put on your pasta, but follow the golden rule: Avoid sauces made with saturated oils and animal fats; experiment with making your own all-vegetable, tomato-based sauce. If you must use oil, try olive oil, which is a monounsaturated oil, and is better for you than the oils that are thick or solid at room temperature. Even then, try to keep the use of oil to a minimum—one or two tablespoons if you're making a few servings from scratch.

Salad

Salad is a perfect complement to pasta. Feel free to try your own favorite mixes of lettuce and vegetables. Be careful of the dressing. Remember that salad is like pasta in that the fattening part is what you put on top. The safest salad dressing is vinaigrette made with a quality polyunsaturated or monounsaturated oil (safflower oil or olive oil are best).

Broccoli

It is wise to include broccoli and cauliflower in your diet at least two days a week. Here's why:

1. Broccoli is high in complex carbohydrates.
2. Broccoli has more Vitamin C than do oranges. (A 1-cup serving of cooked broccoli has 140 milligrams of Vitamin C; a medium-size Valencia orange has 59 milligrams.)
3. Broccoli is rich in beta-carotene—the substance that, once digested, turns into Vitamin A. (A 4-ounce serving gives you about 3,000 I.U. of beta-carotene.)
4. Broccoli is rich in B vitamins, including thiamine and niacin.
5. Broccoli is rich in minerals, including calcium, phosphorus, iron, and potassium. (A 4-ounce serving provides more than 400 milligrams of potassium.)
6. Broccoli is high in water-soluble fiber, the type of fiber believed to be beneficial in reducing cholesterol levels.
7. Numerous studies have shown that broccoli, cauliflower, and related vegetables belonging to the family of plants called *Cruciferae* (including cabbage, brussels sprouts, and kale) are strong anticarcinogens. They produce a class of substances called indoles, which tend to neutralize the harmful effects of carcinogenic agents.

Why You Need Beta-carotene

Beta-carotene is the vegetable form of Vitamin A. Once it's in your system, beta-carotene turns to Vitamin A, and then it's no different from the kind of Vitamin A you get eating meat and dairy products. There is a difference in the way the beta-carotene is packaged: Because it is found in fruits and vegetables, it doesn't come with unwanted fat and cholesterol.

One of the biggest benefits of beta-carotene (Vitamin A) is its power as an anticarcinogen. A recent study at Johns Hopkins University showed that people with high levels of beta-carotene had a significantly lower incidence of lung cancer. Apparently Vitamin A boosts the power of the body's immune defense system. For the same reason, Vitamin A helps fight infectious disease, and it promotes healing. Broccoli is one of the richest sources of beta-carotene, but you can also find it in other dark, leafy vegetables such as spinach and kale, and in yellow-green vegetables such as carrots, squash, and sweet potatoes. It's also in fruits including apricots, peaches, papayas, and melons.

Victory Dinner #2

Favorite Fish Dinner

Fish
(Your favorite fish—steamed, poached, broiled, or grilled)

Fresh Green Salad
(With dash of vinaigrette dressing)

Steamed Cauliflower

Brown Rice

Glass of White Wine

Let's look at the individual ingredients in the Victory Dinner #2.

Fish

The healthiest ways to cook fish are baking, broiling, steaming, poaching, or grilling. Consult a good fish cookbook for the method best suited for the type of fish you have. Remember, the ground rule in preparing fish is to avoid fats and oils.

Obviously, this goes for any sauce you put on fish, too. You should stay away from sauces made with cream or animal (saturated) fats. If you want a sauce or flavoring on your fish, try brushing it lightly with olive oil, then sprinkling on a few herbs. You can also find recipes for low-oil fish sauces, such as ones that are tomato-based.

Cauliflower

Like broccoli, cauliflower is in the *Cruciferae* vegetable family, and, also like broccoli, it contains a long list of beneficial vitamins, minerals, and anticarcinogens. Remember that the most nutritious way to prepare this wonderful vegetable is by steaming.

Brown Rice

Brown rice has a nutritional edge over white rice because all its vitamins, minerals, and fiber have been left intact. Brown rice comes in long- medium-, and short-grain varieties; experiment until you find your favorite type. There is no difference in preparation, however. The easiest ways to cook brown rice are in a heavy-duty pot, rice cooker, or a pressure cooker. Follow the cooking instructions on the rice package.

Whenever Jim Palmer (see page 22) visits Los Angeles, he stays at our home. He's a great cook and delights in preparing dinner for our family. The pleasure is mutual because his chicken recipe is one of our all-time favorites and has become one of our five once-a-week menus.

Roast Chicken

Fresh Green Salad

Chicken alla Palmer
(Roast chicken with Marinade Palmer)

Steamed or Stir-fried Vegetables

Steamed Red Potatoes

Mineral Water
or
Glass of White Wine

Let's take a look at a few tips on how to prepare two of the dishes in Jim's chicken menu.

Chicken

First, wash and remove the skin from 3 whole, boneless chicken breasts (removing the skin reduces the fat content). Cut the breasts in half and pat dry, then place them in Jim's special marinade for one hour in the refrigerator. To make the marinade, in a large bowl combine the following ingredients:

2 tablespoons Dijon mustard

3 tablespoons tarragon vinegar

Juice of one lemon

Two large, pressed garlic cloves

¼ cup chopped, fresh basil

1 teaspoon oregano leaves

1 teaspoon dried dill

½ teaspoon freshly ground pepper

2 tablespoons chopped, fresh parsley

Place chicken in a shallow pan with a rack and bake, uncovered, for 35 minutes at 350° F. After roasting, place chicken boned side down in a broiling pan and broil until golden brown—or sprinkle with paprika without using the broiler, to give it color.

Potatoes

My favorite way to cook potatoes is to steam them for 25 minutes (for small- to medium-sized potatoes; for larger sizes, quarter them first). Or, you can substitute baked potatoes because there is no oil used in the preparation. Potatoes themselves are a wonderful source of complex carbohydrates, and as such they are not fattening. An average-sized potato has only about 100 calories! Potatoes get fattening only when they are cooked in fat and grease or are covered with butter and rich sauces.

Go ahead and put a teaspoon of margarine or yogurt on your potatoes, or sprinkle them with chives or herbs, but stay away from sour cream, cheese sauce, butter, and other heavy oily and fatty toppings.

Victory Dinner #4

The Victory Dinner #4 is very quick and easy; it's low in fat, and is unbelievably good.

California Burrito Special

Two Corn Tortilla Burritos

(Two corn tortillas filled with shredded chicken, lettuce, tomatoes, onion, and a bit of avocado, and sprinkled with shredded Swiss cheese. Top with a dash of salsa, Bragg Sauce, or low-salt soy sauce)

Iced Tea

or

Cranberry Juice Cocktail

(A thirst-quenching 50/50 mixture of cranberry juice and mineral water or Perrier)

These burritos are quick, easy, and very nutritious:

Corn Tortilla Burritos

Heat a corn tortilla in a skillet. Lay it on a plate, and heap on lettuce, tomato, avocado, black beans (see following, BLACK BEANS), onion, a little shredded Swiss cheese, and a little cooked shredded chicken. Then add a few dashes of salsa or Bragg sauce (a tasty no-oil, low-salt sauce available in most groceries).

Black Beans

Beans have a terrific balance of complex carbohydrates and fat, and black beans in particular have a wonderful taste that complements these burritos. It takes a while to cook a pot of beans, so I usually have this dinner when there is time to plan ahead, such as on weekends. Then I cook extra beans, freeze part of them, and have them handy for weekdays when there is less time to cook.

To cook black beans, soak 1 pound of beans in 5 cups of water overnight. Drain the soak water, then add just enough fresh water to cover the beans. Bring water to a boil, then cover and simmer gently until tender (about 1½ hours). If you like, you can also add ½ cup of Mexican salsa a few minutes before the beans are tender, then toss in some chopped cilantro before serving.

"Hold the Steak" Dinner

Baked Potato
(Served with your favorite selection of low-fat toppings)

Artichoke
(Steamed in its own natural juices)

Mixed Green Salad
(With vinaigrette dressing or oil and vinegar)

Mineral Water
or
Cranberry Juice Cocktail
(A thirst-quenching 50/50 mixture of cranberry juice and mineral water or Perrier)

Baked Potatoes

Baked potatoes are packed with nutrients—and only a few calories. They make a terrific dinner when combined with a salad with vinaigrette dressing. If you order this dinner in a restaurant, you can have fun telling the waiter, "I'll have a baked potato and salad, but please hold the steak."

Remember, potatoes are not fattening; it's what you put on them that can be fattening. To keep your potato from becoming a calorie bomb, all you have to do is choose from one of the following toppings:

A little grated Parmesan cheese
A little grated mozzarella cheese
Low-fat cottage cheese and one teaspoon of chopped onions
Chopped garlic sautéed in a minimum amount of olive oil
Chopped green onion
Bragg sauce
One teaspoon melted margarine
Your favorite combination of herbs

Steamed Artichokes

Most cooks complain that artichokes take too long to steam. Here's a way that's fast and tasty:

Wash and snip the ends of two artichokes. Wrap in Saran Wrap, put in a microwave for 13 to 15 minutes, set on high (different microwaves have different powers—experiment to find the optimum cooking time for your model. Also, note that one artichoke takes 7 to 9 minutes.)

You won't need salt, mayonnaise, melted butter, or any other kind of sauce. The microwave seals in the delicious artichoke juices. They're high in potassium and fiber, kids love them, and there are no pots, no pans, no boiling—and no cleanup.

Mixed Green Salad

Try combining your favorite types of lettuce (Bibb, Boston, romaine, spinach, etc.) for a colorful salad. Fresh green vegetables complement the baked potato, and together they provide a nutritious and easy-to-prepare dinner.

What About Dessert?

From my own experience, and from what my family and friends who have followed the Victory Diet tell me, you can actually reduce or eliminate your craving for sweets. It really is true: The fewer sweets you eat, the fewer sweets you crave. It's just like salt or oil or meat in your diet: Once you reduce the amount of sugar you eat, you'll reduce your desire for it.

But how do you wean yourself? One way is to finish your meal with a small sweet that has a powerful, lingering taste. My favorite is a Frazier Mint. They're small and tasty, and a single one after dinner goes a long way.

Try it. Limit yourself to just one bite of sweets; you'll find that after a while you don't even need that single bite.

Another way to eat dessert is to wait until you need that evening snack (more on this in the next chapter). In this category, a good choice is a fresh apple or some applesauce. If you've had dinner at, say, 6:00 and you're hungry at 9:00, a fresh apple or applesauce with cinnamon will keep you happy until bedtime, and it will also cure any morning constipation you might have.

A Few Tips on Getting the Most Enjoyment Out of Dinner

1. Don't overeat. Forget about cleaning your plate because of the starving kids in Bangladesh. Overeating won't help them, and it won't help you.
2. Eat dinner slowly. Chew each bite and savor the flavors and texture of your food. Make your meal last half an hour or more.
3. Avoid distractions. Don't have the TV on, don't read the newspaper. Again, savor your food. Concentrate on its flavor and enjoy it.

4. Keep down the noise. If you turn on the stereo, play soft, pleasant music.

5. Make the dining table attractive. Use place mats or a tablecloth, and cloth napkins.

6. Don't mix heaps of food on your plate, then turn yourself into a human garbage disposal. (I try to stay away from buffet dinners.) Arrange your food on your plate in a tasteful presentation, placing different dishes in discrete areas so they don't overlap. You'll enjoy your meal more, and you'll tend to eat more slowly.

Another suggestion is to eat a different Victory Dinner each weekday evening, then repeat your favorites on weekends. This variety will ensure that you get more than an adequate distribution of vital vitamins, minerals, and proteins.

A reminder: Eating dinner early means you'll wake up hungry, ready for a big breakfast, ready to continue your new eating habits. Eating dinner early also means you may feel hungry before you finally get to bed. Remember, on the Victory Diet you don't deny yourself. If you feel really hungry, you should eat. That's why I devote the next chapter to satisfying and filling snacks.

Pat Boone

Pat Boone is a hugely successful entertainer and author.

Age: 53
Weight at 21: 175 pounds
Weight today: 178 pounds

BREAKFAST

First thing in the morning, Pat has the juice of a freshly squeezed lemon in a glass of water. "My dad has been doing this for years, and fifteen years ago a nutritionist told me fresh lemon juice cleans the liver." Half an hour later he has a high-fiber cereal (sometimes with fruit) and a cup of coffee.

LUNCH

Because of his schedule, Pat usually eats a late breakfast and sometimes skips lunch. When he does eat lunch, he has a fruit salad or green-leaf salad.

DINNER

Pat usually eats a moderately large dinner. He always starts with a big green salad with pine nuts and wheat germ. His most frequent basic recipe is fish or chicken with vegetables and rice. On the road, he usually orders "every vegetable on the menu, rice, and some melted cheddar over the whole plate." He tries to eat dinner no later than 7:00 P.M.

EXERCISE

Pat starts every day with abdominal exercises, and in the afternoon just before dinner he does a hard workout at the health club. He also likes racquetball, tennis, bicycling, jogging, and basketball, which he says is his favorite. "I intend to continue playing full court until I'm seventy at least."

COMMENTS

Pat is another guy who looks twenty years younger than he is. He's a walking example of the real elixir of youth: good eating and exercise habits combined with positive thinking.

◄ ◄ 8 ► ►

And Eat All the Snacks You Want

One of the tenets of *The 7-Week Victory Diet* is: **Never go hungry.** If you feel like having a snack, have one. You won't gain any weight so long as you have the right Victory Snack.

This is an important chapter because snacking is the bugaboo of dieters. It's the potential pitfall for everyone trying to lose weight.

Anyone who has tried to diet and failed knows the pattern. Let's take the case of a guy who's been working hard all day. He knows that he won't be home until 8:00, but he doesn't take time out at work to eat something at 6:00. When he gets home he has a drink or two, a big dinner at 8:30, finishes by 9:30, and stays up to work on a report due the next day. He has another drink and starts working. Ten-thirty passes, then 11:00, and he's getting a little tired. By 11:30 he needs a lift, something to stimulate him. He's ready for temptation.

Let your imagination conjure up the sudden appearance of a well-built, 22-year-old blond woman standing in the kitchen. Assuming you're male, what could be more tempting? Well, I'll tell you. There is something in the kitchen even better, even sexier, even more delicious. It's in the freezer, lying in wait—a pint of Häagen-Dazs chocolate–chocolate-chip ice cream.

Now our friend is a connoisseur of ice cream. He knows you don't just dig into a pint of Dazs' good cold stuff. It's too hard. So he puts the whole container in the microwave and nukes it for thirty seconds. With a tablespoon he now carves the edges, working his way toward the smooth center. He's artistic about it; he's enjoying himself. He's worked hard all day, and he feels he's earned this moment of pleasure.

He finishes the pint, goes to bed, and during the night his body goes to work on the 1,200 calories contained in a pint of Häagen-Dazs. The cream sets the stage for his cholesterol to notch up a few points. His body works overtime breaking the ice cream down to its constituent fatty acids, but there are many more of those little guys than his body needs. The extras get shunted off to the fat cells growing around his girth. By dawn those fat cells are happily overfed, and our friend is well on his way to adding another pound to his already overweight frame.

The way to avoid this kind of temptation is to do with the ice cream what this guy's wife would do with the 22-year-old blond. Throw it out. Go to your refrigerator right now, and throw the ice cream out the door. Throw out everything that looks close to tempting: candy, cookies, cake.

I admit that this act is very hard to perform. In fact, it may be an impossible request to make of your self-discipline without giving you something to take the place of all that junk. On second thought, before you start tossing, go to the store and fill a basket with a healthy selection of fresh fruit: apples, bananas, pears, peaches—whatever is in season. Make sure you buy extra apples. Back home, fill a basket with fruit and set it on display. Make it look attractive, make it look tempting. Now go back to your kitchen. Take out a mixer or food processor; then core and grind some of the apples. Cover the processor tightly, and put it in the refrigerator.

Now comes the fun part. While you're at the refrigerator, pull out all the junk, especially the ice cream. Now go to your cupboards and gather up the cookies and other junk snacks. Gather it all together, and toss it into a large garbage bag. Seal it and get it out of the house *immediately*. Don't keep a little something around "just in case." Have your own Boston Tea Party and *dump it all*. It will really make you feel good. Honest.

Eat All the Snacks You Want and Stay Thin

Snacking is a very important part of *The 7-Week Victory Diet*. Eating the right snacks—all the snacks you want, all the snacks you can hold—will prevent you from feeling hungry or from feeling deprived. You won't be tempted to go off the deep end with a candy bar or ice cream cone, and you'll lose weight, even if you eat all the snacks you want!

Here then is the simple Victory Snack Plan:

Between Breakfast and Lunch

If you eat a full-sized Victory Breakfast, chances are you won't feel like you need a midmorning snack. Remember, you want to save room for a good, medium-sized lunch. On the other hand, you may be one of those hard-working persons who needs a lot of energy to keep going full speed, especially in the morning. If that description fits you, I've got good news: All you have to do to maintain full energy at midmorning is eat another breakfast! Eating a second breakfast is the perfect way to avoid the midmorning coffee and doughnut trap. It's an eating habit used successfully by U.S. Senator John Heinz.

Jack Heinz's Double Breakfast Snack Strategy

United States Senator John Heinz, at 6 feet 3 inches and 210 pounds, is, among other things, one of the top athletes in the U.S. Senate. He's in very good shape, but it wasn't until recently that he found a foolproof way to keep his weight down. Jack's problem was that even though he ate a big breakfast every morning at 7:00, he was always hungry by 10:30. Because he was conscious about his weight, though, he would force himself to avoid snacking. The result: By 1:00 he was famished and invariably ate a huge lunch, which in turn threw off his eating pattern for the rest of the day. The result was that Jack continued to wrestle with a weight problem.

Then he hit upon the perfect solution: the second breakfast! He stocked his office with a supply of the one-serving–sized boxes of Shredded Wheat and some nonfat milk. Now when he's hungry at 10:30, he just eats another whole-grain cereal breakfast. That gives him all the energy he needs to power ahead until lunch, and it curbs his appetite sufficiently to avoid overeating at midday.

Once he started eating a second breakfast, Jack peeled off fifteen pounds, and he did it without any restriction or denial of his eating habits.

I recommend that anybody who has an urge for a midmorning snack do the same. It's just an extension of the Victory Breakfast Strategy of eating as much as you want—eating all you can hold—in the morning.

Between Lunch and Dinner

A medium-sized lunch sometimes leaves you hungry in midafternoon, and because you want to avoid eating a big dinner, I strongly recommend that you eat an afternoon snack.

The perfect food at this time of day is fresh fruit—an apple, pear, banana, or chunks of cantaloupe or honeydew melon. All are relatively easy to eat at your desk or to carry in a handy bag for a quick snack on the go. Fruit on a relatively empty stomach will pep you up with instant energy. It's a great way to sail at top speed right through the 3:00 doldrums.

Between Dinner and Bedtime

You'll sleep better and enhance your weight-loss program if you go to bed on a relatively empty stomach, but that doesn't mean you can't enjoy an evening snack if you feel hungry. A good evening snack is fresh homemade applesauce. It tastes great, is great for you, and is easy to make. All you do is purée some cored apples in a food processor, then sprinkle on a little cinnamon, but don't add sugar. You won't need it.

Another suggestion for an evening snack is a bowl of either Shredded Wheat or Nutri-Grain cereal with skim milk and perhaps a cup of camomile tea. So long as you don't overdo it, you'll still wake up ready for a big breakfast.

Fruit is also a good evening snack. The best type to eat in the evening is a variety with a high water content, such as peaches (try adding some skim milk and a dash of honey— delicious), tangerines, grapes, nectarines, or melon. Fruit with a high water content will digest faster, and you won't go to bed on as full a stomach.

Closeup on Fruit: The Perfect Snack

Fruit is the perfect snack food because it tends to quench your appetite. A study by the Veterans Administration Medical Center in Minneapolis discovered that xylitol, one of the sugars found in fruit, actually causes food to pass more slowly through the digestive system, thereby reducing appetite. In an experiment, they gave the control group plain water before lunch, and they gave another group water with xylitol. Without any prompting, the xylitol group ate an average of 230 calories less than the control group. When the researchers then fed the experimental group solutions of regular sugars and sucrose, their appetites went right back up.

Fruit, then, is not only satisfying as a between-meal snack; it also helps to reduce the amount you eat in the meals that follow your snacks. In other words, eating fruit can help you lose weight. It's like a magical solution: You eat more, and weigh less.

Remember, though, it's not a good idea to eat fruit with a meal or as a meal. Fruit eaten with a meal tends to give you gas, and the fruit sugars don't combine well with other foods (although many people can add fruit to their cereal with no side effects). The only exception to this is grapefruit before breakfast. Grapefruit seems to agree with nearly everyone in the morning.

Fruit as a snack, though, is perfect. Nearly all varieties of fruit are terrific sources of key vitamins and minerals. For these reasons, fruit for a snack gets high marks as a true wonder food.

Apples: The Wonder Fruit

Apples are one of the best snack fruits you can eat. Because they are crunchy and require chewing, apples are satisfying between meals. They also are high in a type of fiber called pectin. Like all fiber, pectin increases your regularity and decreases your risk of such diet-related diseases as colon cancer. Studies have also shown that pectin can actually reduce cholesterol in people suffering above-average levels.

Alternate Victory Snacks

Although fruit is far and away the best snack food you can eat, there are other foods you can munch on that won't add pounds and will give you a little variety.

Popcorn

The good news is that popcorn is good for you as a source of both complex carbohydrates and fiber. But you have to watch out for the goop that often goes on it: butter and salt. You simply should not eat popcorn with either of these added.

If you do need to add something, try a little melted margarine (avoid brands made with hydrogenated or partly hydrogenated oils and choose a type made with polyunsaturated oil). But give popcorn a try with nothing on it. It's easy to get used to. In fact, like any new eating habit, once you do get used to it, you'll find the old stuff will taste greasy and salty.

Raw Vegetables

Many vegetables taste great raw, and because of their crunchiness they make satisfying snack foods. Broccoli and cauliflower are at the top of the list, as are carrots. Be careful, though, to avoid those sour cream or mayonnaise dips often served with raw vegetables.

The Drink Dilemma

One of the between-meals pitfalls that millions of Americans fall into is the trap set by the soft-drink industry. Canned soda is a billion-dollar business, and with that kind of money it's not surprising we are bombarded with ads telling us to join the Pepsi Generation and that "Life Goes Better with Coke." And for those watching their waists, the appeal to buy the so-called diet drinks is even more persuasive.

The soft-drink industry has been absolutely brilliant in their use of the word "diet." It's amazing how many people they sucker in with this one.

We had lunch recently with a young fashion model who makes $500 an hour posing for *Vogue* and *Mademoiselle*. Not surprisingly, we got on the subject of food and nutrition, and she confessed that although she is careful with her diet, she nevertheless drinks eight to ten diet Cokes a day. Eight to ten! She's been lulled into thinking that, with the word "diet" on the can, she's okay.

What she doesn't realize is that the "diet" can is full of salt, caffeine, and additives such as phosphoric acid and even coal-tar derivatives.

She also doesn't realize that the artificial sweeteners in diet drinks are creating in her system a desire for sweets and sugar that is not satisfied by the diet drinks. She has a craving for real sweets, and drinking that quantity of artificial sweeteners is only setting her up to go off the deep end with even more harmful dessert foods. One study involving 80,000 people showed that those fed artificial sweeteners actually gained weight because their appetites were enhanced.

If you're looking for a satisfying drink between meals, you should try mixing fruit juices—my favorites include apple, cranberry, and white grape juice—50/50 with mineral or soda water. They're light and refreshing, and you'll find them more thirst-quenching than any canned soda.

There's one other drink, too, that deserves not just special but extraordinary mention. It's the most important drink you can put in your body.

The Wisdom of Drinking Water

I've already stated that the best way to start your day is with a glass of warm lemon water. That should be only the beginning.

The 7-Week Victory Diet recommends that you drink five glasses of water a day. Water helps your body lose weight by flushing from your kidneys harmful waste products that keep you unhealthy. Here's a story that indicates the importance of drinking water. Rick Ridgeway, world-class mountain climber, was among the four who were the first Americans to climb K2, and the first ever to do it without the aid of bottled oxygen. The only way he could achieve such a feat was by *drinking 5 or more quarts of water a day*. Because of the lack of oxygen at such a high altitude, his excessive breathing caused an abnormal expulsion of carbon dioxide, which in turn set up a Ph imbalance in his blood. The only way to overcome this was by substantially increasing his consumption of water. The water flushed out his kidneys, restored the Ph balance in his blood, and allowed him to climb to very high altitudes.

I'll admit Rick's is an extreme example, but it is nevertheless a lesson for the rest of us who remain at or near sea level. By drinking lots of water, we get the same benefits as the high-altitude mountaineer: Our kidneys are flushed clean of harmful waste products.

You should drink five glasses of water a day, and you should drink them between meals. Drinking water with meals dilutes your stomach juices and impairs digestion. A glass of the juice–

mineral water combination with lunch is okay, but you should limit it to just one.

Here are some additional water tips:

1. Reduce the risk of dehydration by drinking *before* you feel thirsty, especially if you're working out. Drinking a glass of water fifteen minutes before you start a workout is a good practice to follow.
2. The higher the altitude at which you are exercising, the more frequently you should drink.
3. Drinking a glass of water an hour before dinner readies your digestive juices for your meal.
4. Don't substitute sugar or diet soft drinks for water.
5. World-class athletes have found that it's best not to drink any of the carbonated mineral waters while exercising. Good old plain water works best.

◄ Part III ►

THE VICTORY EXERCISE PLAN

Dr. Barbara Guggenheim

Barbara received her PhD from Columbia University in art history and was assistant professor of art at Rutgers University. She headed the primitive art and American painting department at Christie's and was a member of the board of the New York Academy of Art. Barbara is currently president of the Art Tours of Manhattan and is recognized as a major international art consultant.

Age: 40
Weight at 21: 128–132 pounds
Weight today: 114 pounds

BREAKFAST

Every day Barbara has a glass of fruit juice and a toasted bran muffin without butter. She has oatmeal at least four days a week.

LUNCH

Barbara alternates three basic lunches: tuna salad, sardine salad, or chicken salad. For a beverage, she drinks mineral water. On weekends she sometimes indulges in a couple of slices of pizza.

DINNER

Barbara has three basic dinners: fish, chicken, and pasta, each served with a salad. She eats no red meat and no fried food. Occasionally she has a glass of wine and a fruit tart for dessert.

EXERCISE

Barbara works out five days a week, alternating between aerobics, stretching, and yoga.

COMMENTS

You may have noticed that Barbara's weight today is well under her weight at age 21. When I asked her about this, she confessed, "At 21, I was out of shape. I was overweight and had no muscle tone." Barbara is one example of someone whose target weight is right at the weight she has worked to maintain *since* she was 21.

Barbara has an interesting schedule. She spends work days either with clients or in her office. At 6:15 P.M. she religiously works out for forty-five minutes. She has dinner at 8:00. Then, if she's not with clients, she returns to her office and works from 9:30 until 1:00 A.M. Barbara's late hours are the reason she gets away with eating dinner so late: For her, the time between eating dinner and going to bed is about the same as for someone who eats at 6:00 and goes to bed at 11:00. She says her late-night stints are when she gets most of her creative work accomplished. Barbara also feels strongly that without her exercise regimen, which gives her an enormous amount of energy, she would be unable to do the kind of difficult research and creative work necessary for her to excel in her field.

Good Exercise Habits: Companion to Good Eating Habits

Eating the right foods at the right times is only half of winning the food fight. The second—and equally vital—half is exercise.

Stated simply, you've got to exercise to reap the full benefits of *The 7-Week Victory Diet*. But that doesn't mean you have to do anything complex, time consuming, costly, or painful. Like the diet portion of this book, the exercises I recommend are targeted toward *making things as simple as possible*.

Almost everyone knowledgeable about nutrition and health physiology agrees that exercise should be an important part of any weight loss plan, and everyone agrees that good eating and exercise habits are the two legs on which good health stands.

Consensus, however, stops there. Many plans advocate a minimum of twenty minutes of exercise a day strenuous enough to give your heart a real workout. Others say you need a full hour to get optimum benefits. I agree that strenuous exercise, the kind that gets your heart rate up to a level that gives you a solid, aerobic workout, will yield top health benefits. But I disagree that this kind of exercise is what you ought to tackle right away, especially if you've never exercised at all or have not exercised in many years.

After all, how many of us have both the time and the discipline to exercise vigorously an hour a day? The Victory Exercise Plan is built around a more realistic belief: that if you are one of the 80 million Americans who are currently sedentary—meaning you don't do any regular exercise, and you probably never have—you're simply not going to lace on some jogging shoes and pound the pavement for five miles, or hop onto the aerobic dance floor and whip your heart rate up to 150 beats per minute and keep it there for half an hour.

The only result you get from too much exercise *too soon* is discouragement. If you try to get into serious aerobic exercise all at once, you'll get sore, you'll get injured, or you'll start coming up with excuses or distractions why you can't continue. *Physicians and Sportsmedicine Magazine* published a survey that showed that nearly 80 percent of Americans who start an exercise program drop it within six months to a year.

To beat this high drop-out rate, the Victory Exercise Plan is designed in two steps. The first easy step—explained in Chapter 10—is to begin a program of low-volume exercises designed to get you in shape and at the same time get you used to using your body.

When a low-volume level of exercise becomes comfortable, you'll discover you're in the exercise habit and will want to move up to the next phase, high-volume exercises. Once you get in the high-volume exercise habit, you'll enjoy better posture and more stamina. And the chances are that your blood pressure will be lower and you'll be more alert. In other words, you'll look better, feel better, and sleep better.

The only thing I can't guarantee is that you'll have more money. But with all those other benefits, chances are you'll do better at work, too.

Before and After: My Twentieth High School Reunion

If I ever had doubts about the importance of leading an active life that embraces a daily dose of good exercise, they were laid to rest at my twentieth high school reunion.

It was one of the more interesting days of my life. Do you remember the girl for whom you would have crawled on your knees just to touch the hem of her skirt? Or the guy who would have caused you to faint if he had ever said hello? What do they look like twenty years later?

In my case, I didn't recognize her. Someone had to point her out because she must have weighed close to 200 pounds. The twenty years since graduation had taken a frightening toll. Many of the women and men, all between the ages of thirty-seven and thirty-eight, and most of whom I remembered as at least reasonably thin and healthy, were already overweight, out of shape, and equally difficult to recognize.

Not everyone was over the hill, though. In fact, some of my old classmates didn't look too different from the way they had at age seventeen. I started talking to some of them, asking what they did for work and play. Sure enough, the ones who were trim were also active. They played tennis and softball, or they went hiking with their kids.

The overweight seemed to have a hangdog look. Standing there, we were all gazing into a mirror reflecting twenty years of life, twenty years of decision and indecision, of action and inaction. From the looks on their faces, I suspected many of my overweight classmates were gazing in the mirror with a kind of wistful melancholy, wishing perhaps they could go back in time and do it all over again.

Aiming for Your Target Weight

The irony of this reunion was that everyone there was capable of going back in time. If they could know how easy it is to change eating habits and how important it is to acquire a few exercise habits, they could remake their bodies to look something like they did nearly twenty years before. Not exactly the same, of course—some guys had genes that made their hair fall out at an early age—but by and large everybody could regain the figure of their youth.

The 7-Week Victory Diet allows you to go back in time. With the Victory Diet's eating and exercise habits, everyone can have a figure similar to the one he or she had at age twenty-one (that's if at age twenty-one you were in reasonably good health and were not overweight or underweight).

We all know that the best way to achieve something is to fix your eye on a specific, tangible goal and to start working for it. If you were a healthy weight at twenty-one, your ultimate weight-loss goal should be to weigh what you did then. Emphasize that word *ultimate* because you'll get to your goal in stages.

To help you visualize this ultimate target weight, fix in your mind an image of what you looked like at age twenty-one. If you have one or two full-length photos of yourself from this age, study them and keep them handy as a reference or an inspiration. At least once a day, or whenever you're tempted to slide back into an old unhealthy habit, try to "see" yourself as fitting this image. The more you practice this technique, the easier it will become, and you'll soon find yourself moving toward that target weight.

The Scale God

You should own a quality scale to measure your weight, but you shouldn't bow down to it every morning. First, bathroom scales, even good ones, are notoriously inaccurate. Second, your weight can vary from day to day depending on such factors as how much water you've been drinking.

Make sure you purchase a quality scale. The balance-beam kinds are best. Place it on a hard-surface floor, and don't move it around. Moving changes the calibration.

Try weighing yourself only once a week. In this way, you keep track of your general weight loss, but you don't get hung up worrying about minor day-to-day fluctuations.

Jack Valenti and John Tunney, who are both profiled in this book, weigh themselves religiously every morning and trim down on their meals if they are inching over their ideal weight. That's okay if you're already down to your target weight, but if you're struggling to get to that weight, daily weighing is an unnecessary distraction.

In addition to your bathroom-scale weight, it's helpful if you know your body-fat weight—that is, the percentage of your weight that is made up of fat.

To understand why this is important, let's go back in time and look at what our bodies were like at age twenty-one. If you were like most people at that age, you were at your proper weight not only because you were trim but also because you were fit. In other words, you not only looked lean, but under that trim skin was fit muscle. At age twenty-one you were still young enough, and you probably still got enough exercise, so that your body fat was close to where it should have been.

Our bodies are primarily composed of bones, muscles, and fat; body fat is simply the measure of that percentage of our total weight that is composed of fat. It's also a critical measurement of just how fit we are. Here's an example: Let's assume we have two men, age twenty-one and forty-one respectively. Both are 5 feet, 10 inches, both weigh exactly 165 pounds. You can tell by looking at them, though, that the young kid is in much better shape. Why? It's not just age. It's because the older man has stopped exercising, and as a consequence has 25 percent body fat where the younger man has only 10 percent. Even though they weigh the same, the older guy has fat starting to marble through his tissue, whereas the younger one has only lean, hard muscles.

It's getting harder and harder for the older man to maintain his 165 pounds, too, and you can bet the day is just around the corner when he starts looking like the tire man in the Michelin ad (in fact, he is in a very temporary transition period where he's out of shape but hasn't yet started gaining weight). That's why your goal, your target weight, is not only to weigh on the bathroom scale what you did at age twenty-one but also to have close to the same percentage of body fat that you had then.

And what percentage is that? In all likelihood, at twenty-one you were reasonably fit and consequently were close to your ideal level of body fat. Most experts agree that the ideal level is about 15 percent body fat for men and about 20 to 25 percent for women (varying a little with their body shapes). Women get a higher allowance than men because their body shapes are designed to have a higher relative percentage of fat tissue.

Here, then, is your true target weight: *You want to weigh what you did at twenty-one with a body-fat measurement of 15 percent for men and 20 to 25 percent for women.*

How, then, do you measure that body fat?

Fat Floats and Muscle Sinks

There are two popular ways to measure body fat. One is the caliper-pinch technique, but it is almost totally inaccurate. The far more accurate method is the water-immersion technique.

To get your body fat measured with the caliper technique, you go to some place like your local health club where a trainer takes a set of plier-like calipers, grabs a fold of skin at a specific location on your arm, and measures its thickness. If your health club's got the latest model machine, the calipers are hooked to a computer that already has your vitals: age, height, weight. The calipers are then applied to other points on your body: waist, pectorals, thigh, stomach, calf. The computer then accesses these data and spits out your percentage of body fat.

In my case, the computer-generated figures just didn't look right. I was told I had a body-fat measurement of 19 percent, so I decided to go back the next day. I had the same measurements, and this time the figure came out at 10 percent body fat!

A friend had his body fat measured by calipers at two different locations: The results varied by more than 50 percent.

So I decided to have my body fat measured by the water-immersion technique. This system is based on the simple fact that fat floats and muscle sinks. If you could remove one pound of fat from your body and plop it into a tank of water, it would float. Take a pound of muscle, and it would sink.

It's the same if you plop your body into a tank of water, which is what happens when you use the water-immersion test. If you're fat, you float. If you're lean and muscular, you sink. Measuring just how much you sink or float versus how much water you displace is a much more accurate measurement of the percentage of your weight that is fat.

With the water-immersion method, my body-fat reading came out at 13 percent.

If you want the most accurate reading of your percentage of body fat, I strongly recommend you use the water-immersion method. You can find immersion tanks at most good health clubs.

How often do you need to get measured? Only two or three times, really. You should get measured before you start this program so that you have a yardstick by which to measure your progress. Then you should get measured again as you near your target weight. For reasons I'll discuss next, if you are following the right eating habits and the right exercise habits, and your weight is getting close to target, your percentage of body fat is also getting close to target.

Body Fat Follows Target Weight— If You Exercise

Remember that previous example of the two men age twenty-one and age forty-one who weighed the same but had different percentages of body fat? Their case illustrates how people can be the same weight and height, yet one can be fit and the other out of shape. I also mentioned it was a safe bet the older guy wouldn't remain at his present weight much longer. Here's why he's going to get fat:

As he starts to get out of shape, fat will begin to replace muscle in his body (muscle cannot turn into fat, but it can decrease, just as fat can increase). As fat increases, he won't burn as many calories in his system because fat doesn't require as much fuel as muscle in order to maintain itself. You can bet, though, he's not going to cut back on his calories to keep up with his lowering energy requirements. Instead, he'll continue to eat as he always has, and he'll start getting fat.

If our 41-year-old had kept up with an exercise program, however, he would have maintained his muscle tone. Those muscles would have continued to burn more calories, even when he was sitting around doing nothing. In medical terms, the rate of his basal metabolism would have been higher, and in nonmedical terms, the man would have stayed lean and trim.

That's why anybody who is forty-one and still weighs what he or she did at twenty-one is almost certain to be in good shape. It's possible the person could be in the transition zone—like the 41-year-old in our example who hadn't yet started gaining—but it's unlikely. That's why I maintain that nearly everybody who is more than forty and at his or her target weight has good muscle tone and, consequently, a low body-fat reading

That's why you don't need to have your body fat measured more than twice. If you're at or close to your target weight, and you're following the right eating and exercise habits, you'll be within safe body-fat limits.

How, though, can you get to that target weight if you are thirty, forty, or fifty pounds over it?

By the Inch It's a Cinch; By the Mile It's a Trial

If you're less than fifteen pounds over your target weight, then set your sights on getting down to that weight. If you're more than fifteen pounds over, though, you need an interim goal. You need some mark you can aim for that isn't such a long throw away.

If you've got more than fifteen pounds to lose, then divide your weight-loss program into a series of goals, each about seven to ten pounds apart. When you lose the first ten pounds, stay there for a little bit, getting comfortable with your new eating and exercise habits. Then move on to the next ten-pound segment.

Another tip: If you are more than forty years old and you are more than twenty pounds over your 21-year-old weight, you'll be a lot less frustrated if you set your sights on a more realistic goal. Whether you're a man or woman, take your 21-year-old weight, add ten pounds, and make that your target weight.

Remember, the trick to losing a lot of weight is not to try so hard all at once that you get frustrated.

 Winner's Circle Profile

Helen Gurley Brown

As editor of *Cosmopolitan* magazine (which now has nineteen foreign editions), Helen is often seen on television talk shows and is the author of two top-selling books: *Sex and the Single Girl* and *Having It All*. There is a chair in her name at the Medill School of Journalism at Northwestern University.

Age: 65
Weight at 21: 109 pounds
Weight today: 105 pounds

BREAKFAST

Every morning Helen follows the same breakfast routine. As soon as she gets up she has a glass of fresh carrot juice. She then completes her morning exercise routine and has breakfast: Nutri-Grain cereal with a peach or banana. She doesn't drink coffee or tea.

LUNCH

Most days Helen eats lunch at her office desk. She has a single favorite menu she eats most days: tuna salad topped with green beans, red pepper, mushrooms, and tomato. On weekends at home she often prepares a *giant* salad that includes iceberg lettuce, cabbage, toasted sunflower seeds, shredded Swiss cheese, chopped tomato, chopped fresh parsley, cooked green beans, and small amounts of either chicken, tuna, or shrimp. She also likes brown rice mixed with heated skim milk, raisins, Equal, and Butter Buds (she calls it her "fake rice pudding").

SNACK (about 6:00 P.M.)

Helen usually has a snack about this time of day. Her favorite is a few slices of skim-milk mozzarella cheese with a sliced apple.

DINNER

Because of her business, Helen often eats in restaurants, and she tries to order the same thing as much as possible: fish. She avoids a first course and hors d'oeuvres unless it's consommé. Then she asks for broiled fish whenever she can, preferring sole, flounder, or salmon. She also enjoys a vegetable with the fish, so long as it doesn't have a cream-laden sauce.

When she is at home, Helen doesn't eat anything until just before bedtime, usually

(continued)

about midnight. She then has a bowl of Kellogg's All-Bran with raisins, chopped almonds, and skim milk. She sometimes has a dish of diet Jell-O or a bunch of grapes.

EXERCISE

Helen works out seven mornings a week for about thirty minutes. She exercises again for about ten minutes before going to bed.

COMMENTS

Helen Gurley Brown calls herself a "beyond-redemption workaholic." She spends several hours of every Saturday and Sunday writing at her typewriter, reading manuscripts or competitors' magazines, and dictating office memos and letters. She says her diet routine may sound austere but that it really isn't. She eats large portions: On weekends she will have a giant serving of her "fake rice pudding," and at night as much as a half pound of grapes.

Helen feels that her exercise regimen helps her to stay slim: She's missed only two days of exercise in the past twenty years. She also credits her health, fitness, and enormous vitality to eight hours of sleep each night, careful eating habits, a capacity to get lost in work, a glass of wine now and then, no caffeine, no drugs (not even aspirin), and no cigarettes. Helen says she rarely has a cold, never misses work, and she walks *everywhere* (she lives in New York City).

Low-Volume
Exercise

The past ten years have brought an explosion in the number of people who jog, walk, swim, bicycle, play tennis, or attend aerobics classes. It's fantastic to see so many people working out, but unfortunately the number of Americans who have tried exercise and dropped out is greater than the number who have stuck with it.

Take the case of Susan, who works in my office. She's extremely bright, in her late thirties, and has two kids and a husband who helps around the house but also works. She's in a responsible managerial position and has moved quickly up the company ladder.

Holding it all together—job, husband, kids, house—has been a real strain, however. Not long ago it was taking a toll on Susan, and she was getting out of shape. Not the kind of person to let something slide, though, she decided to take action.

Susan later told me what happened. She decided to sign up at her local health club for the aerobics class taught by Bambi Goodbody. Bambi taught two advanced aerobics classes every morning, then rode her ten-speed bicycle all afternoon unless she was working on her tan. The way Susan described her, Bambi had a body that wouldn't quit but a brain with about nine fewer gears than her bicycle.

Susan was apprehensive. She knew she'd feel more confident if she at least looked right, so she went out and spent $200 on Lycra leotards and dance shoes. When she showed up for the first class, she saw that the other members of the class were mostly women. The few men present looked sheepish; Susan guessed that they were embarrassed knowing that everybody thought they were in the class just to look at Bambi (which was probably true). Everybody seemed fit—as though they had been doing this for a while.

The music started, and so did the bouncing, clapping, and yelling: Woo-woo, ya-ya, woo-woo-woo. Susan found it was kind of fun. She got into it, and ten minutes later she was breaking a sweat. Twenty minutes later she was breathing hard but managing to keep up. At thirty minutes, she was starting to get worried. Could she make it through the whole forty-five minutes?

Susan is a tenacious woman, so she set her mind to the task and pulled it off. She was very pleased until the next morning when she couldn't get out of bed. Her husband helped her, supporting her by the arm as she limped to the shower. Ten minutes of hot water got things loosened enough to get both the kids and herself ready for the day. She made it through work, but two days later, when it was aerobics time again, she couldn't bring herself to go. The leotards and dance shoes remained in the closet, and Susan joined the ranks of America's exercise dropouts.

Susan didn't realize that the place to start an exercise program is not on the aerobics floor but in her own home.

When I explained to her that the volume of exercise to start with is not a forty-five–minute workout but a ten-minute daily ritual of easy-to-perform exercises she can do right on the carpet next to her bed, she was all ears.

Susan started my low-volume exercise program, and after two weeks she noticed her posture improve. She was lighter on her feet and, best of all, her back pain stopped nagging her. The only thing she regretted was the $200 she blew on the workout gear.

The American Dilemma: The Bad Back

I read once that at some point in their lives, 80 percent of all adults in the United States experience some form of lower back problem. My own informal survey puts the figure closer to 100 percent; everybody I know has had some kind of back problem at some point. Bad backs, stiff backs, sore backs, sore butts: it's a list of ailments that keep the orthopedic doctors and chiropractors in this country in business.

When I was about fourteen years old, my lower back started hurting, so I went to our family doctor. He took one look and told me I had hyperextended knees, which meant that when I stood up straight my knee joints locked beyond a normal position. As a result, the back of the joint pushed out slightly, stretching my hamstrings and pulling down on my back muscles. The family doctor prescribed adding a quarter of an inch to the heels of my shoes, which did relieve quite a bit of the pressure.

Meanwhile, I was very active in sports—football, track, basketball, skiing, and surfing. In those days there was no such thing as running shoes. In fact, I used to go down to the beach and run three miles on the hard sand in my bare feet.

All this time, though, I had lower back pain. All I could do was learn to live with it. After about ten years of running in my bare feet, I decided to try wearing tennis shoes (this was still before running shoes). My back *still* hurt. Then about ten years ago the running shoe craze hit, and I tried every possible model. My back *still* hurt.

By this time, I was fifty-five years old. I'd been to orthopedists; I'd tried massages; I'd even tried acupuncture. Nothing worked.

I was sick and tired of living with a sore back. It got so I couldn't sit still because of the pain. The more I skied, the worse it got. The harder I ran, the worse it got.

Finally I went to my neighborhood back doc, a guy named John Hertz (as in the word *pain*). He wanted to know what I'd been doing, and when I described the sports I pursued he said, "Quit running."

"But I've been running for about thirty years."

"Quit running, or your back's going to hurt forever. Pretty soon you're not going to be able to get out of bed."

"What do I do for exercise?"

"Start riding a bike, start swimming."

"That'll fix my back?"

"Hard to say, but at least it won't hurt it any more. If you want to do something that might really make a difference, though, I know someone who can help. He's a yoga instructor, a guy named Larry Payne."

I paused for a moment to reflect. "Hertz and Payne. Maybe I'm seeing the wrong guys."

The Key to a Strong Back Is a Strong Stomach

"You have weak stomach muscles," said the yoga instructor. "That's why your back hurts."

"My stomach muscles aren't weak. I jog, I surf, I ski. Look at my stomach. There's no flab on it."

"Lie down on your back. Now bend your knees and give me forty half sit-ups."

I did what he said and couldn't believe it when, no matter how I strained, I couldn't get past eighteen.

"Your stomach is the center of your body," he continued. "Your entire posture, including your back muscles and vertebrae, depends on it for form and strength."

He told me to start doing half sit-ups every morning, along with some other stretching and strengthening exercises.

"What the hell," I thought, "nothing else has worked."

For two weeks I did sit-ups like crazy. Then a funny thing happened. I started to stand straighter. And I couldn't believe it—the back pain started to subside.

I did more research on abdominal muscles and learned that for exercise purposes the stomach is divided into three regions: upper, middle, and lower. The lower portion is from your pubic bone to just below your belly button, and is the area where most people need attention. The middle abdominals are the muscles around your belly button, and the upper abdominals are those below the bottom edge of your rib cage.

I also researched every stomach exercise I could find, and I eventually put together a set of exercises that gave a thorough workout to all three abdominal regions and helped my back at the same time. I started incorporating them into a morning workout ritual. After thirty days of this regimen, my back pain was almost completely gone!

Only those of you who suffer from chronic back pain can understand what this means. I'm talking about forty years of pain that after thirty days was 90 percent gone. Forty years! It's like a blind person given sight: The world suddenly comes to life, and everything seems to sparkle.

To say the least, I was sold on half sit-ups. I gave up running and decided to stick with my morning abdominal exercise routine plus a few stretches combined with a little swimming and bicycling.

My morning abdominal and stretch workout took only ten minutes to perform. It was a simple, low-volume program without the yelling or hype and cost of an aerobics class. It was a program that got my blood circulating in the morning, put a real bounce in my day, and—very important—didn't involve pain.

"No Pain, No Gain" Is Just Plain Nonsense

People shout it on television, health clubs extol it, the aerobics teachers echo it: "No pain, no gain." It's just plain B.S. It's a negative, antiexercise phrase that has turned a lot of people away who otherwise could benefit from a low-volume exercise routine.

Another vehicle that I believe turns people away is the ads showing sweat-glistening bodies with sinewy muscles or killer figures pumping iron and running marathons. People see those kinds of ads and figure they have no chance of looking that good, so why bother.

Well, you do have to bother. Forget the tanned and muscled models, forget the people who tell you to go-for-the-burn to get any health benefit from exercise. *Low-volume exercise works*.

How do I know? Foremost is my own experience. I've been doing my morning abdominal routine for seven years now, and I've told you how it has helped my back, my posture, my overall muscle tone.

Several recent studies have also confirmed that low-volume exercise benefits your health.

A University of Minnesota coronary prevention study involving 13,000 men showed that those who performed about half an hour a day of light to moderate exercise reduced their risk of heart attack by a third.

A Harvard study had similar results, showing that you get

significant health benefits regardless of how much or how fast you burn calories, so long as you get *some kind* of exercise that burns them.

In other words, you *do* benefit from low-volume exercise, and you benefit in a big way. So it's time to stop making excuses, and start doing a few minutes of low-volume exercise every day, starting with a morning abdominal routine. Some of you may prefer to do these exercises in the evening, just before you go to bed. That's okay—follow whatever pattern best fits your own schedule.

The Low-Volume Exercise Program: The Morning Abdominal Routine

In addition to the "no pain, no gain" hype, there's another common exercise fallacy: A lot of people think you have to exercise a long time to see any results. That just isn't so. If you follow these low-volume abdominal exercises every morning, you'll be able to see a difference in only two weeks.

There may be a time at the beginning when trying to do even a few half sit-ups is going to be a little difficult. Any exercise you haven't done before always carries a measure of difficulty, but have faith that the routine gets easier. In fact, any discomfort you feel will stop only seconds after you do your final sit-up. Furthermore, I don't want you to start with so many exercises that you'll be sore the next day.

Forget the super jocks and forget the workout kings and forget the 20-year-old Bambi Goodbodies. You *can* gain with *no* pain if you undertake a low-volume exercise regimen.

Abdominal exercises will firm your stomach and straighten your back. With a tighter stomach, you won't feel so hungry all the time. Your posture will improve. Man or woman, these exercises will reduce shoulder slump, back hump, and forward neck lean. You'll stand straighter, relieving back pain, neck pain, and back-related headaches.

Waist Away

Lie on your back, knees bent and slightly apart, feet on the floor. Now suck in your stomach toward the floor as far as possible. Hold it for two seconds—two thousand one, two thousand two—then push out on your stomach, hold for two seconds, suck back in. Repeat twenty times.

Butt Tightener

Lie on your back with feet on the floor about twelve inches apart, and with knees bent and apart. Raise your butt off the floor, bringing your knees together, and hold for three seconds. Lower butt to floor, letting knees fall apart. Repeat ten times. After you're comfortable with this exercise, increase the work on your upper abdominals by raising your shoulders slightly off the floor, bringing chin to chest as you raise your butt.

Hip Twist

Lie on your back, knees bent, feet on the floor, arms out to either side. Bring your knees all the way to the floor on the left, and move your head to the right. Keeping your knees together, move them all the way to the right and your head to the left. Repeat twenty times.

Back Stretcher

Lie on your back with legs out straight. Bring your right knee up as close as possible to your chin and hold for ten seconds. Let it down, and bring your left knee up and hold for ten seconds. Repeat ten times, then bring both knees up as close as you can to your chest and hold for ten seconds.

Pay-Off Crunch

Lie on your back, knees bent and apart, feet flat on the floor, hands clasped behind your head. Press your chin to your chest and do a half sit-up, keeping your lower back flat on the floor and bringing your knees together as you come up. Almost touch your elbows to your knees, and make sure your knees stay pressed together. Then lower yourself down, widening your elbows and spreading your knees. Repeat twenty times.

The trick with the Pay-Off Crunch is to build up to as many repetitions as you can do. This takes time. You may be able to do only ten each day of the first week, and if that's your maximum, *hold it there*. The second week, try for fifteen, then twenty in the third week.

When you get stronger, you can consider two variations to the Pay-Off Crunch.

1. As you do the half sit-up, lift your feet off the ground four inches.
2. As you do the half sit-up, cross your elbows so they are extending toward the opposite knee.

Horizontal Bicycle

Lie on your back, with legs out straight and hands clasped behind your head. Do a half sit-up and at the same time, bring your right leg up as though you are riding a bicycle. Bring your left elbow as close to your right knee as possible. Repeat this movement, but this time bring your left leg up and your right elbow over. Do this twenty times.

The Horizontal Bicycle and the Pay-Off Crunch are the two key abdominal exercises. Don't do too many of these at first. Build up slowly. Remember, you don't have to feel any major pain to get the gain of a low-volume workout.

Cat Stretch

Get on your hands and knees, then suck in your gut so your back arches like a cat's. Hold it for a few seconds, then push down and arch your back, hold for a few seconds, repeat. Try to do twenty—this is a great exercise for back strength.

Yoga Pose

Get on your hands and knees, touch your forehead to the floor, close your knees, and stretch your arms all the way back. Remain in pose until whole body feels relaxed.

More Tips for Getting Rid of Back Pain

Invest in a Good Pair of Running or Walking Shoes

Wearing a pair of running or walking shoes as your everyday shoes is a wonderful way to reduce back pain. They give more support than dress or casual shoes, they're more comfortable, and, when you walk or run, they absorb more of the shock. All of this takes strain off your back.

If you have a job that keeps you standing for any length of time, you probably know how painful it can be to wear regular dress shoes, no matter how well made or how expensive. Personally, I can't do it. That's why I suggest you try to wear running or walking shoes as much as possible.

Some running shoes are getting spiffy enough to pass as dress shoes. I have a black pair that I've worn to cocktail parties and fancy restaurants. I've even worn them with my blue business suits to meetings. I've yet to see anyone raise his or her eyebrows—they don't even notice.

A few people are beginning to get wise. Walk a midtown street in New York, and you'll see men in business suits wearing running shoes and carrying briefcases large enough to hold a pair of dress shoes for office meetings. Women especially are walking to work in running or walking shoes instead of the body-deforming heels that used to be standard attire.

John Williams: Rx for Back Pain

On a typical concert night, John Williams, conductor of the Boston Pops, stands on the podium for three hours. Wearing formal dress shoes, it's a back-breaking task. I wasn't surprised to learn he had serious back pain.

As an old pal, I told him there was a good chance his stomach needed strengthening, and I suggested he try a routine of low-volume abdominal exercises. He took me up on it, and in no time his back was better. Now he follows the program religiously.

I also recommended he wear better shoes, which he does. He can't go so far as wearing black running shoes on the podium, because people can see his feet, but he sure wears them at rehearsal. Between a strong stomach and a good pair of shoes, his back pain has almost completely disappeared.

Use an Extra Pillow When You Sleep

There's another way to take pressure off your back that few people, except pregnant women, seem to know about. It's the trick of putting a pillow between or under your knees when you sleep. Here's how you do it: If you sleep on your side, put the pillow between your knees.

If you sleep on your back, the pillow goes under your knees.

I can hear what you're thinking: Okay, Mr. Wizard, I twist and turn, going through these positions several times a night. How am I going to keep a pillow in place?

Don't worry. After a few nights, you'll automatically move the small pillow when you shift without waking up.

I started this habit a couple of years ago, and now I really miss it if I'm in a hotel and I don't have an extra pillow to stick between my knees. At home I use a soft circular foam pillow about eighteen inches in diameter and six inches thick, and I often take it with me when I travel. I know that sounds ridiculous—akin to Linus and his blanket—but believe me, after you discover how much better your back feels in the morning, you'll be willing to drag a small pillow around the world.

The Hot-Shower/Cold-Shower Trick

Have you ever soaked in a hot tub at a ski resort, climbed out and dived into a snow bank, then jumped back in?

If you have, you know that it feels absolutely fantastic. You probably don't have a hot tub and snow bank in your backyard, but you can get the same results by finishing your hot shower with a quick cold one.

I've been doing this every morning for forty years, and believe me, I'm hooked. Here's what it does for me:

1. It closes my pores. This is important, especially if I've had a very hot shower. And if I've just finished a hard workout, closed pores keep me from continuing to sweat.
2. It helps my blood circulation.
3. It's great for my skin. Whether you're a man or a woman, you can benefit from good skin tone. This is why most high-fashion models have learned to finish their showers with cold water.

Hot Tubs, Saunas, and Massages

Hot tubs, saunas, and massages all make you feel great, but don't count on them to burn off, sweat off, or rub off calories. It just doesn't work that way. You can get wrapped up in mud, towels, cellophane, herbs, and leaves, and none of it will make you lose weight. Even if you steam in a sauna until you're pruned out, the most you'll do is lose a pound of water that you'll gain right back at the nearest drinking fountain.

That's not to say tubs and saunas don't have their place. Hot tubs especially can be a great way to stretch and loosen morning muscles. Pregnant women should avoid hot tubs and saunas, however, because high temperatures can cause injury to an unborn child.

You've Got to Walk Tall

I told you earlier how my twentieth high school reunion was a real eye-opener. One of the biggest shocks was the number of people who had let their posture deteriorate. Invariably, the ones who were stoop shouldered were the ones who also had a defeated look. When you asked how things were going, they were the ones who said, "Not too bad—I guess."

My classmates who had maintained a straight back and squared shoulders, however, were the ones with a twinkle in their eyes. They were the ones who said, "Things are great."

I can't impress upon you how important it is to discipline yourself to stand straight. It's a habit that will do wonders to bolster your confidence and boost your self-esteem. That in turn will give you a more positive outlook, and it's been shown time and again that those who think positively maintain better health.

When I think of good posture, I'm reminded of a guy I've known for thirty-five years. Those of you in skiing will recognize Stein Erickson as the Norwegian Olympic gold medalist who became a major influence in American skiing. Stein is in his early sixties, but he looks today just as he did thirty years ago. It's uncanny. And one major reason is that the man stands arrow-straight. If someone asked me how tall Stein is, I would say 6 feet 2 inches. The truth is, he's 5 feet 8 inches, but I *think* of him as being much taller. His straightness gives him added stature.

I know there are many exceptions, but as it is with overall health and nutrition, I've found most people who are successful are people who also have good posture. They're people like Earl Jorgenson, president and CEO of Jorgenson Steel, who at age eighty-eight exercises every morning for a half hour, eats well, and has a twinkle in his eye. Needless to say, the man stands straight as a plank.

How can you improve your posture? The best place to start is with your stomach. To stand straight, you've got to have a well-toned abdomen. After you've followed the morning low-volume abdominal program for a couple of weeks, start to remind yourself to hold your back straight whether standing or sitting. Develop an inner watchdog that gives you a little pinch every time it catches you slumping.

More Great Low-Volume Exercises

Swimming

Swimming is probably the greatest exercise there is. It's a terrific low-volume exercise if you swim at a slow rate, and it's a fantastic high-volume workout if you crank up the pace. It's also not stressful to your joints, ligaments, and muscles, and it's the safest workout you can follow if you have back problems.

If your back is really weak, or if you're recovering from a back injury, here's the way to take all the pressure off your back while you swim. Buy an inexpensive waterskiing belt, and put it on with the padded side on your belly. Then with mask, snorkel, and fins, float on your stomach. Your back is supported completely by the flotation in the ski belt. Now you are ready to start swimming laps.

If you really want to feel that you've returned to the womb, put a tether on the ski belt, hook it to the end of the pool, and start swimming slowly against it.

After a couple of weeks, you'll find your overall muscle tone improving and your back strengthening. You may find yourself strong enough to start swimming without the waist support.

Walking

For years walking has been pooh-poohed as legitimate exercise by people who don't think you burn enough calories to make it worthwhile. When you walk a mile, for example, you burn about the same number of calories you gain by eating a tablespoon of mayonnaise.

Another way to look at this, though, is that if you walk that mile every day and do nothing else (including not eating any extra mayonnaise), at the end of a year you will have burned enough extra calories to lose ten pounds. Now does it seem worth it?

Burning calories, though, is only one of the benefits of walking. I find it to be a great low-volume exercise to do after eating. It helps you to lose weight by speeding your digestion as well as by burning calories. One study showed that the number of calories the body absorbs after a meal can be cut as much as 15 percent by taking a walk. My favorite time to walk is after dinner (another reason for eating an early dinner!).

Walking is also a perfect antidote for frustration. At the end of a difficult day's work, it's much healthier to vent your pent-up emotions rather than to sleep with them. There's something in the metronomic nature of walking that relieves stress, and stress has been shown to be a principal agent in the deterioration of a person's immune system. Walking actually helps you to ward off illness.

My Mother-in-Law

Recently my mother-in-law slipped and broke her arm rather badly. At age seventy-five, the orthopedist wisely told her that the only way she would mend quickly was to get plenty of exercise and to eat healthfully to strengthen the calcium in her bones. Supplements alone wouldn't do it.

The trouble is, the doctor didn't tell her anything specific. She knew I was working on this book, so she asked me for a copy of the manuscript. Soon she was eating a big oatmeal breakfast and taking a brisk thirty-minute walk five days a week.

My mother-in-law has been forty pounds overweight for as long as I've known her. But in three months of following the Victory Diet, she dropped from 155 pounds to her target weight of 115 pounds. Now this is a woman who has been overweight for fifty years! She's a woman who has tried everything, even enrolling in the Pritikin program where she lost weight only to gain it back when she couldn't follow the Draconian restrictions. Today she looks like a new woman, she feels 100 percent better, and her arm has healed rapidly. On top of that, she has finally admitted—after my twenty-six years of marriage to her daughter —that I might just have a smidgen of intelligence after all.

Edgar Bronfman

Edgar is chairman of the board of Seagram Corporation and the principal owner of Du-Pont. *Forbes* magazine puts his net worth at close to $1.3 billion, which I'd guess is about a billion short.

Age: 58
Weight at 21: 155 pounds
Weight today: 165 pounds

BREAKFAST

Edgar has the same breakfast nearly every day: half a grapefruit, a large bowl of whole-grain cereal, and one piece of whole-wheat toast. He doesn't drink coffee.

LUNCH

Edgar eats a medium-sized lunch, usually fish or chicken and salad.

DINNER

Edgar eats a very light dinner, usually pasta or fish. He has a glass of wine with his meal, but skips dessert. He rarely eats red meat.

COMMENTS

Edgar Bronfman is an extremely well-known and successful businessman and is one of the

(continued)

richest men in the world. For most of his life Edgar was not very athletic. In fact, at age twenty-one he was ten pounds underweight. Recently, however, Edgar broke his leg in three places while skiing. His injury required major surgery, with bone grafted from his hip. His orthopedic surgeon, an excellent sports physician, told Edgar in no uncertain terms that he would have to concentrate on an extensive therapy program or he wouldn't regain full use of his leg.

In the old days Edgar would have been in a cast for six months and in rehabilitation another six months. Edgar took the doctor's therapy program to heart, though, and five months later he was not only back on his feet but also looked better than he had in years.

Edgar maintains his exercise program to this day. To heal his leg, he began two forty-five–minute workouts a day. Now that his leg is back to normal, he's dropped back to one workout per day: Every morning he pedals his stationary bicycle twenty minutes, then works his arms and legs with weights for twenty-five more minutes. This is a man who all his life did very little exercise.

"I've never felt so good about the way I feel and look," he told me. "If I miss more than a day of my exercises, I get irritable and need a workout fix. I think that ski accident was a blessing in disguise."

Here's a man who could afford anything in the world. Until recently, though, he more or less ignored his health. Now he realizes that it's the most valuable thing a person can own.

High-Volume
Exercise

Have you ever noticed how lean people move and fidget more than overweight people? Even sitting in a chair, lean people are always tapping a foot or squirming in their seat. It's as though they feel compelled to move.

In fact, they *are* compelled to move. Because they have a high percentage of muscle tissue in their bodies, they are constantly burning energy, even while they are sitting. They are like powerful engines that at idling speed can't wait to start revving.

Time and motion studies have proven that in the course of a typical day lean people move around much more than heavy people, even when they're doing nothing! Why? Because they've got muscle that is burning energy, muscle that is begging to be used. They've got high metabolisms.

And despite what you may think, the reason they have high metabolisms is not because they were born that way. Some people tend to be leaner than others—everybody has a different basic body shape—but it's absolutely wrong to use your body shape as an excuse because *you can change your metabolism*. All you have to do is eat right and exercise right.

Studies have proven that people who exercise regularly have higher metabolisms than those who are sedentary. Conversely, fat people burn energy slowly. Fatness is a vicious cycle: The fatter you get, the less energy your muscles burn and the more the food you eat turns into fat.

The best way to break that cycle is through common-sense exercise—exercise that won't discourage you, won't bore you, and won't give you any excuse to give up.

That's why I recommend that you start with the low-volume exercises described in the previous chapter. Remember, even low-volume exercise burns calories, improves muscle tone, reduces stress, and helps increase immunity to cancer and heart disease.

After you've followed the low-volume program for a few weeks or months, your muscles will start to strengthen. You'll be burning more energy, even when you're sitting still. You'll begin to acquire the behavior of high-metabolism people. You'll want to move around more. You'll want to exercise more.

The Victory Strategy of low-volume exercises naturally leads to the high-volume program. When should you start high-volume exercises? If you were fifteen to thirty pounds over-weight when you began, and if you follow the low-volume program, you'll be ready to take on high-volume workouts in about six weeks. If you are more than thirty pounds overweight to begin, you should check with your doctor to make sure that a more strenuous program will not cause harm.

Sweat Once a Day

Several years ago, I spent a couple of days working on a project with Lynn Swann (profiled on page 150). Swann was the all-pro flanker for the Pittsburgh Steelers, and he is considered one of the greatest wide receivers of all time.

Swann is in magnificent condition, and I had a long conversation with him about staying in shape. He said the trainer for the Steelers had devised a basic rule-of-thumb to help everyone on the team to stay in shape off-season.

The rule was: *Every day make sure to exercise enough to work up a sweat.*

I agree with that 100 percent. Produce a good sweat, and you're going to lose weight and stay in shape.

How to work up a sweat? Any of the high-volume exercises will do it, but so will low-volume workouts. If you follow the abdominal routine for twelve minutes, chances are you'll break a sweat.

High-Volume Exercise

High-volume exercises get the blood pumping through your system, which in turns cleans out toxins from your muscles and arteries and gives your heart and lungs a good workout.

Equally important, high-volume exercises can be fun. If you are going to stick with an exercise program the rest of your life, the fun factor is essential. Otherwise, you get bored and give up. For the same reason, it's also important to rotate exercises. Try swimming one day, jogging the next, bicycling after that.

Before you start any high-volume exercise, though, make sure you warm up and stretch. Stretching beforehand is absolutely essential to prevent injury.

Another essential is to drink plenty of water before and during high-volume exercise. Drink one glass about fifteen minutes before you start your workout, and drink while you exercise. Contrary to popular belief, this will not make you sick or give you a sideache. During high-volume exercise, water helps keep your body's core temperature within safe levels, and it also helps flush lactic acid and other wastes from your muscles. Be sure to drink plain water, though; it's better than any juice, energy drink, or carbonated mineral water.

You should never eat a meal just before high-volume exercise. Your body requires considerable energy and blood to digest food, and this is energy and blood that also are required for high-volume exercise.

I've seen this mistake made many times in ski areas. Somebody in a hurry to get on the slopes will eat a small breakfast. By noon they're famished and eat an enormous lunch. They go back to the slopes feeling lethargic and they ski clumsily. It's no surprise that statistics from the National Ski Patrol records show most skiing accidents and injuries occur within one hour after lunch.

Recommended High-Volume Exercises

Swimming

Swimming is one of the best high-volume exercises. It offers a great workout for your heart, lungs, and muscles, and it is virtually stress-free for your joints and ligaments. Unlike running, swimming is a full-body workout: Studies of competitive swimmers have shown that 80 percent of their forward motion comes from their arms and shoulders.

You can change swimming from a low-volume to a high-volume workout by varying your strokes, using pull-buoys or swim fins and increasing the speed at which you swim. Be sure to stretch before you swim, though, to reduce muscle tightness and improve flexibility.

Bicycling

Bicycling is great because it's easy on your knees, ankles, and back. It can be a dangerous sport, though, so you should always wear a helmet even if you're riding only a block to pick up a newspaper. I know someone (sans helmet) who was killed doing just that.

Make sure your bike is adjusted properly because this can save your neck and back a lot of grief. Try a mountain bike or dirt bike instead of a racing bike. The tires are fatter, so you'll get more exercise pedaling. And unless you're a serious biker —one who rides 25 miles a day or more—you'll find a mountain bike or dirt bike much more enjoyable and easier to ride. They're a lot safer, too, because you sit straight and have more control. Stretch before and after you ride to loosen your muscles and decrease the risk of injury. If the weather is always bad where you live, buy a stationary bike. It's worth the investment and is a good way to watch the morning news!

Water Exercises

There is a better way of exercising than going to an aerobics class or jogging and beating yourself to death. It's called fitness through water exercise. Water exercise was originally conceived as therapy for injured athletes and others. When Mary Decker Slaney suffered an injury to her Achilles' heel in the 1984 Olympic trials, she immediately began water therapy to keep in shape while the heel improved. Ten days later she got back on dry land and set a world record in the women's 2,000-meter run.

Lynn Williams, an exceptional Canadian runner, had a similar experience preparing for the 1984 Olympics. Only a few months before the games, she suffered a stress fracture. She transferred her on-land training to the pool, "running" across the pool, using the same motion of arms and legs to keep her afloat. Two months later she set her personal best in the 3,000-meter run and went on to win an Olympic bronze medal. She was so impressed with her recovery, however, that she decided water exercising was the best training, whether she was injured or healthy.

Both athletes and general exercise enthusiasts have discovered that water exercise is the most comprehensive, injury-free form of aerobic exercise there is.

Lynn Williams has found her ideal water exercise to be a 30-minute workout three times a week. For those 30 minutes, she "water jogs," taking about 2½ minutes to get from one end to the other of a 25-meter pool. Forward movement, obviously, is not important.

Some people find it awkward to stay upright or afloat. You can solve this with a Wet Vest, a flotation "life vest" that holds you upright while you water jog. But they're not cheap—the last time I looked, about $110—but then neither are some athletic shoes.

A number of water-exercise books are on the market, but

you can also find classes at your community pool, YMCA, or local health club. A good instructor will lead you through a warm-up, aerobics, and a cool-down.

You can perform other dry-land sports in the pool, too. Swinging a tennis racquet underwater is a good way, for example, to keep your tennis arm in shape without injuring your elbow (just be sure to use an old racquet). You can swing a baseball bat, too. Ray Wershing of the San Francisco 49ers practices place-kicking in water.

Aerobics

Aerobic exercise is now the second most popular form of regular exercise in America (the first is walking). It's easy to learn and it's fun. It's also a very strenuous workout, so remember the lesson of Susan in Chapter 10: To avoid discouragingly sore muscles or injury, you should be moderately fit before you attempt to complete an aerobics class at full speed. Remember, you can get injuries from aerobics (a California study found that 43 percent of aerobics students and 76 percent of aerobics instructors have sustained some kind of injury during exercise). Because of the free-form nature of the movements, and the jumping and bouncing, it's easy to strain a muscle, ligament, or tendon, especially if you're out of shape or not warmed up. A good way to work up to aerobics is to follow the low-volume exercise program (see page 119) for six weeks before you start aerobics.

You can develop an aerobics program to follow in your home, or you can join a class. If you have never done aerobic dance exercise, it's probably best to join a class. Ask about the instructor's credentials, and make sure you begin in a program suited to your level of ability. Wear a good, comfortable pair of aerobics shoes, and don't do aerobics on a cement floor.

Joining a class is fun, too. Many people find it easier to keep a high energy output if they have others to exercise with.

Weight Training

Some aerobics gurus maintain you can't get a real cardio-vascular workout lifting weights. Pat Riley, however, head coach of the L.A. Lakers, told me that the only thing you need to remember to get a good workout on weights is to go for less weight with more repetitions.

You don't have to pump iron, however, to benefit from weights. A Nautilus (or similar machine system) workout is excellent for your posture and overall muscle tone. Stay away from free weights, though, because with them it is much easier to hurt yourself, especially your back. Be sure to stretch before and after your workout.

Jogging

Jogging is what comes to most people's mind when they think of exercise. It's a very good high-volume exercise because it requires only a pair of shoes and some running shorts, and you can do it just about anywhere. Running-related injuries are very common, however. In fact, a recent study at the Long Beach Memorial Medical Center found that, at any given time, 44 out of 100 "casual joggers" (twenty miles or fewer a week) were recovering from some kind of running-related injury.

To avoid running injury *you must warm up first*. The low-volume stretches in Chapter 10 are fine as a prerunning warm-up. Make certain you stretch for a minimum of ten minutes. Then start off at a very slow jog. Continue slowly for several minutes until you can feel your leg muscles start to loosen and your breathing quicken a little. Then slowly pick up the pace.

Running on dirt or grass absorbs a tremendous amount of pounding that on harder surfaces such as asphalt goes straight to your shins, knees, and hips.

Another tip for avoiding injury is to wear good shoes. The most important factor in choosing the right pair of shoes is finding the brand that fits you best. You can do that by going to a running store and trying on as many brands as they have. Don't be fooled by price, either. *Runner's World Magazine* says that above about $35, the additional protection you get in shoes is probably minimal. It's also important to retire shoes when the rubber cushioning in the heel or the sole becomes fatigued. Running on shoes that have lost their bounce increases your chance of injury.

Remember, running can be hard on your back, especially if your spine is slack or weak. Following a routine of low-volume abdominal exercises will help reduce or eliminate any back pain you may get from running because strong stomach muscles keep your back straight, thereby transferring weight directly through your legs to your feet.

If you're considering taking up jogging but have never done any previous exercise, check with your doctor first and be sure to follow the low-volume program for six weeks before hitting the pavement.

Court and Team Sports

Racquetball, tennis, basketball, volleyball, hockey, and soccer are all excellent high-volume exercises, provided you warm up beforehand and cool down afterward.

Walking and Hiking

Walking is one of the workouts I include as both low-volume and high-volume exercise because walking can be a terrific workout. To get aerobic benefit you simply walk at a brisk pace, about three miles an hour. This will get your heart rate high enough to give your cardiovascular system a good workout.

Walking has a very low risk of injury. It's soothing and relaxing and great to do at the end of the day when you need to unwind. All you need is a good pair of shoes, which makes walking a good exercise for travelers.

Like running, you'll find walking more comfortable if you keep your back straight, and you'll find that easier to do if your stomach is strong. I recommend you adopt the low-volume abdominal routine regardless of whether you follow a high-volume program or not.

Walking is something a lot of people should add to their daily routine. Next time you have to go somewhere nearby, consider budgeting enough time to walk. Walk to lunch, or park your car a distance from your office and walk.

Another excellent time to take a walk is after dinner. Walking after eating is a great way to aid your digestion and lose weight. It's also another reason to try to eat dinner early.

Hiking is an even better workout than walking. Whether you have a pack or not, ascending and descending a trail at a good steady pace will keep your heart rate above 120 beats a minute. Hiking is a great antidote for stress, too. What better way to get rid of worries and concerns than to hike them away along a scenic trail?

Outdoor Adventure Sports

The primary attraction of most high-volume exercises is that they are not boring. That's true in spades for what I call outdoor adventure sports.

If you find an outdoor adventure sport that you get hooked on—so that you can't wait until the next time you can get out and do it—I guarantee you'll not be overweight. Everyone I know who is an avid skier, surfer, mountain climber, kayaker, windsurfer, or backpacker (and that is a lot of people), is lean, healthy, and strong.

The great thing about outdoor adventure sports is that they are so thrilling and so much fun that you begin to build your life around them. You consider yourself a "skier" or a "climber" just the way you're a "personnel manager" or a "sales rep." The sport becomes as much a part of your life as your job.

Being hooked like this is the ultimate in exercise and fitness. But don't go into it lightly. Most of these sports involve varying degrees of risk; if there is ever a place where you absolutely have to approach an exercise with the guidance of an expert and the okay of your doctor, outdoor adventure sports is it.

Outdoor adventure sports take time. Often it's most of a lifetime if you want to be really good. But that's the whole idea: to find an exercise or sport that will keep you in shape and that will hold your interest for the rest of your life. And when you get hooked on an active outdoor sport, the rest of your life will probably be lengthened by years. Sports such as these really can be your personal source of renewal and energy.

Lynn Swann

All-American at USC and all-pro wide receiver for the Pittsburgh Steelers, Lynn is an ABC sportscaster (and also an expert amateur tap dancer).

Age: 35
Weight at 21: 178 pounds
Weight today: 173 pounds

BREAKFAST

Lynn eats the same breakfast every day: half a grapefruit, a bran muffin, and two bowls of oatmeal; he also has coffee.

LUNCH

Lynn has a light chicken salad or tuna sandwich with either fresh juice or a glass of skim milk.

DINNER

Although Lynn eats an NFL-sized dinner, he rarely eats red meat. He does eat rich desserts, though, including calorie bombs like chocolate soufflés, cream caramels, and ice cream with cognac sauce on top. He hardly ever drinks hard liquor but does enjoy a glass of wine at dinner.

EXERCISE

No matter where he is, no matter what he's doing, Lynn does 300 sit-ups every morning. He also alternates running, bicycling, and a hard game of tennis, trying to do each of them a couple of times a week.

His travel schedule is hectic, and if he misses his outdoor workout, he always gets in his sit-ups.

COMMENTS

Most successful people have taken the time and the effort to figure out an eating and exercise program that works for them. Sometimes, though, we can't always stick with the program. When that happens, anybody in good health has invariably learned to make up for the imbalance. In other words, within certain limits, eating and exercise habits are in a kind of equilibrium: a slight abuse in one area can be compensated for in another.

That's just what Lynn does. He sometimes eats dinner late, and he often pigs out on sugar-bomb desserts. But he also does 300 sit-ups a day, and he works out extremely hard in sports such as running and bicycling.

Lynn would find it easier to stay in top shape if he were into *all* the balanced habits of the Victory Diet (notice that he does follow my breakfast and lunch guidelines), but I'm not going to fault this guy: He's in killer shape.

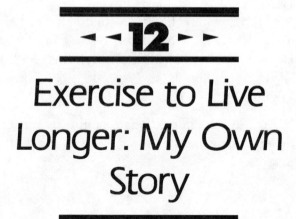

Exercise to Live Longer: My Own Story

In the past ten years several long-term studies have shown that regular exercise reduces your chance of suffering such illnesses as heart disease and colon cancer. There's also growing evidence that exercise can help you handle stress—that it's a great way to externalize all the pressures and worries we suffer in our hectic lives. Before those studies ever came out, though, I found from my own experience how important exercise is to health.

How I Built Up a Successful Business and (Just Barely) Kept Up My Health

When I married at thirty-two, I was careful about what I ate and drank. I exercised regularly and, as a consequence, was still able to fit into the same size clothes I had worn in college.

Less than two years after my marriage, business pressure caused me to lose sight of my priorities. I started to gain weight and to lose my muscle tone. My health problems stemmed from my effort to go into business head first. I was trying to build a big operation from scratch in a very short time.

At the time I was married I had no money, no job, not even an occupation! I was desperate. We were surviving only on the part-time money my wife, Peggy, was bringing in as a model. More than anything I wanted to be a success and to provide for my wife and future family, but where could I start?

A few years earlier I had worked in a real estate office and was toying with the idea of getting back into that industry. One morning while I was waiting in the unemployment line I noticed in the *Wall Street Journal* an ad for a shopping center for sale in Phoenix. They wanted $10 million for it. I still can't figure out what made me do it, but on a whim I clipped the ad, pasted it to the back of a postcard, and wrote in longhand, "Send me a setup. I'm a principal."

I didn't know until later that the postcard was received by the Del Webb Corporation. They had about seventy-five replies to the ad, but mine was by far the most eccentric, so they figured I was some off-the-wall millionaire. They wrote back and said two of their representatives would travel to Los Angeles to meet with me.

At that point I had absolutely nothing to lose. But what to do? I couldn't meet them in the clapboard shack Peggy and I were renting for $75 a month. I needed an office. But where? How?

I remembered an old school chum who had become a successful lawyer and worked out of a very fancy office in Beverly Hills, so I called and asked if I could borrow it for a couple of hours. He couldn't believe it when I told him what I was up to, but he agreed to lend me the office.

A week later the Del Webb people came out for the meeting. I was careful to wear blue jeans, a sweater, and tennis shoes (that's all I had anyway): I had to keep up my image of an eccentric millionaire. It was one of those days when I felt on top of the world, when everything clicked. I was in great shape (I'd had plenty of time to exercise like crazy each day), and my physical stamina seemed to transfer into mental energy. The Del Webb people gave me all the information I asked for, and I told them I would get back to them in a week.

I thanked my buddy for the use of his office, went home to my shack, and stared at the photographs of this huge shopping center. They were asking $10 million, with an existing first deed of $6 million at 6 percent for twenty-five years. The center was showing an annual income of $60,000. What if I could get some investors to go in with me on this thing? I got a piece of paper and worked up some figures. I decided I would give potential investors 10 percent per annum return on their money, so that meant I could offer Del Webb a $600,000 down payment. Then I would propose they carry a $2.4 million second deed at 6 percent for twenty-five years. What the hell, I thought, I've got absolutely nothing to lose. I called them and made the offer. A few days later they called back, said I had a deal, and shortly afterward a contract arrived in the mail at my buddy's law office.

There was just one detail separating me from owning a $10-million shopping center: $600,000 cash. The biggest thing going for me was that I had nothing to lose. I went to Duplicate Photo in Hollywood and for $5 got 100 eight-by-ten black and white glossies of the shopping center. I got twenty-five three-ring binders for $1 each and some plastic covers for a penny apiece. Then I sat down and with my one-finger typing skills pecked out the proposal and outline of the deal. I had the sheets mounted in plastic sleeves for a penny a sheet, and put together two dozen attractive brochures.

Now I had to use my brochures to raise $600,000. Suddenly things changed. Now it was no longer a deal where I had nothing to lose. Now I had an emotional stake in seeing it through. I had absolutely nothing else going for me as a career.

I was desperate, and I told myself I had to make this deal or else.

I dropped my daily exercise program and started working mornings, days, evenings, and nights. I called everyone I knew who had become any kind of success, and I called everyone they knew. Nothing happened. The clock was ticking; Del Webb wanted their down payment. I was nervous.

That's when I started eating. At night, after dinner, when I would pore over my list of prospective investors, I would snack to help dissipate the nervous energy. Then, as the nights lengthened, I would snack to keep awake. When I did eat a meal, I consumed whatever was in front of me. Food no longer mattered to me.

And neither did exercise. Instead of getting outside to jog away my frustration and tension, I was trying to eat it away.

After three weeks I started to gain weight. I went from 165 pounds to 175. It still didn't matter because almost out of the blue I signed my first investor for $25,000. By the end of that breakthrough week, I had two more for a total of $100,000.

I kept working like crazy. My weight inched up, but so did my investment portfolio. I got $200,000, then $300,000—halfway! The Del Webb Corporation was screaming for their money, though. I got an extension, then another. I was up to $400,000, but time was out: they wanted the money or no deal.

I couldn't hand them any of the investors' money because I had promised everyone if the deal fell through they would get every penny of their money back, with interest.

Then my attorney pal told me I could give Del Webb a promissory note because if the deal did fall through, I was judgment proof: I didn't own anything anyone could claim. I pulled an amount—$40,000—out of the air and sent off a note for that amount. They accepted it; I had more time.

I also had a few more pounds around my girth: I was up to 185 pounds. Now it was showing. My face looked heavier, I didn't stand as straight. My wife started making comments, but

I didn't listen. With still a few weeks before the deadline, I got the investment kitty up to $500,000. It looked like I was there.

Then things went dead. I couldn't get another penny out of anybody. I couldn't believe it. My health was now in terrible shape. I was up to 190 pounds. I was fighting bouts of depression, something very unusual for me. I was also getting edgy, flying off the handle at people, even at my wife. Where was my spirit, my optimism? Finally my wife decided it was time to talk.

In her quiet yet assertive way, Peggy pointed out that I was losing sight of what really mattered.

"It's not important whether you have that shopping center or not. We'll always make out okay."

"What do you mean?"

"I mean, it's not worth it if it costs you your health."

I knew, of course, she was right. I wouldn't be providing for her, for our future family, for anybody, if I dropped dead from stress. I had been at this thing twenty-five hours a day, seven days a week, nonstop for eight months. I decided to slow down. I started taking time to get outside and jog on the beach. I stopped snacking on junk food and got back to my simple and nutritious eating patterns. I lost ten pounds, started standing straight again, got back the bounce in my walk.

I had only two days left, though, before deadline, and I still needed the last $100,000. There was only one hope—a rich doctor with whom some friends had put me in touch. I arranged a luncheon meeting. When I showed up, my heart sank: The guy was drunk.

But it didn't matter. I felt good. I had things in perspective. I was walking with a bounce, and I was talking with a bounce, too. The doctor didn't say much during the whole luncheon; he just kept ordering drinks. I finished my pitch and went home. I figured the whole thing was over. It was funny—I didn't feel too bad. I had given it my best shot; no one could deny that. And, thanks to my wife, I still had my health.

The next day I also had my money. The doctor called back, sober this time, and said he was in for the $100,000. I was the owner of a $10-million shopping center! The funny thing is, I'd never seen the property. I'd never had enough money for a plane ticket to Phoenix.

Exercise to Live Longer

Today, twenty-five years later, I still own the Chris-Town Shopping Center, and it's the centerpiece of my company, one of the most profitable shopping center development companies in the United States. I still have my health, and I still fit into the same size clothes I wore in the unemployment line. One of the main reasons is that I still exercise every day.

I am absolutely certain daily exercise has helped me handle stress and, in turn, has helped me maintain my health. In fact, I am certain daily exercise will help me to live longer. That's not just an off-the-wall opinion, either, but a fact corroborated by several research projects, one of the most interesting of which is a ten-year study of 17,000 Harvard alumni aged thirty-five to seventy-four. The study compared exercise habits with heart-attack rates. The results showed conclusively that the people who exercised regularly had fewer heart attacks. It also showed that the higher the level of exercise, the less the risk of heart attack, all other factors that could be measured (such as smoking, illness, hypertension) being equal. Those persons who exercised strenuously at activities such as bicycling, jogging, and tennis had up to 35 percent fewer heart attacks than those who were completely sedentary.

In a nutshell, the study showed that those who exercised more lived longer. Regular exercise improves your health, decreases the negative impact of stress, decreases the risk of heart attacks, and decreases your chances of suffering other severe illnesses such as colon cancer.

The verdict is in: Exercise—*even a little each day*—can help you live longer. You don't have to be a triathlete jock, either. All you have to do is adopt a few low-volume exercise habits, building up to the point where you can add two or three high-volume workouts per week. It's as simple as that. The opportunity for increased longevity is yours, here and now.

Let's see specifically how exercise can help you live longer.

Stress—The Silent Killer

I've noticed in the business world that the person who can handle stress is usually the one who makes it to the top. Most CEOs I know have learned the fine points of stress management. They know how to handle pressure, how to externalize it —in essence, how to cope.

Inability to handle stress makes you less effective. You get tense, your work habits get frantic, and you lose your ability to make calm, deliberate decisions. You also become more difficult to work with because stress can cause moodiness and irritability.

Knowing how to reduce stress can also affect your health in big ways. High blood pressure—caused in large part by stress —afflicts about 40 million people in this country. The majority are businesspeople with stressful jobs. Many of them will die prematurely from heart attacks.

Stress is the silent killer. It insidiously undermines your health, weakening your body's immune system, and leaving you more exposed to common colds, viruses, and even diseases as severe as cancer.

That's why when I was first scrambling to make my business a success I got so many colds. Stress, combined with a poor diet and no exercise, was wrecking my immune system and my health in general. Once I returned to simple eating habits and took enough time to exercise a few minutes a day, I had more energy, I got fewer colds, I had a more positive outlook, and, in the long run, I got more work done.

Exercise—Rx for Stress

A few years back a popular book on stress divided people into two kinds of stress-coping personalities: *A* types and *B* types. You may have read the book, or, if not, you've probably heard about *A*-type people. They are the ones who are always checking their watches, who never have quite enough time to get everything done. Their blood pressure rises in traffic jams; they get frustrated standing in lines.

If any of this sounds familiar, there's a good chance you can do something to improve the way you handle stress. This can be a big challenge. To change your personality takes commitment and perseverance far beyond what's required to change lifelong eating and exercise habits.

There is one thing you can do, though, that I know for certain will improve your ability to handle stress in your life, and it fits right into *Win the Food Fight*. That one thing is exercise.

Let's say you've had a tough day at your job. You come home, and the kids are fighting and yelling. That's got your spouse in a bad mood, and he or she is taking it out on you. What do you do?

Many people would feel sorry for themselves and feel that they deserve some kind of relief from their problems. Many people would go mix a couple of stiff drinks and maybe munch down some potato chips and dip at the same time. But that's no real relief; that's no solution to the problem.

What you really need to do is go to the closet, put on your running shoes, and jog a couple of miles. Or put on your walking shoes and go for a brisk walk. Or ride your bicycle or go swimming. Take your family along—they'll enjoy it, too. Anything to get you out, get your heart pumping, and get the tension out of your system. The metronomic rhythm of running, walking, or cycling will free your mind and help you relax. The exercise will clean your muscles of the stress you've felt all day.

A half hour later you'll all come home feeling 100 percent better.

If there were any way to measure such things, you might learn that the stress relief from your exercise improved your health enough to add a day or two to your life span. And if you were to exercise every time you felt stressed, those days might add up to months, and even to years.

Exercise to Live Longer

The evidence that exercise prevents certain cancers is starting to come in. A study in Los Angeles County discovered that out of 2,950 cases the risk of colon cancer in men diminished as the level of physical activity increased.

Harvard University determined that women who were athletic in college and continued an active life after graduation were less likely to develop cancers of the breast and reproductive systems.

Despite all the research being done, I believe medical science is just beginning to learn the role exercise plays in stress management, and how reducing stress increases your immunity to everything from colds to cancer.

Exercise reduces blood pressure and the risk of heart disease, and it may help prevent colon cancer. That's just the tip of the iceberg. Once you start exercising regularly, you'll know intuitively that your body is doing a better job warding off illness and disease. You'll just be able to feel it. Like changing your eating habits, adopting exercise habits is addictive. You'll feel so much better, you'll be hooked. If for any reason, such as illness or injury, you have to stop exercising for a few weeks, you'll be itching to get back to it, to get that "good feeling" again.

You will be in the winner's circle.

◄ Part IV ►

THE 11-IN-7
VICTORY PLAN

Sherry Lansing

Sherry is a very successful motion picture producer (you might remember her huge recent successes, *Fatal Attraction* and *The Accused*). She was the first woman in entertainment history to become president of a major studio—20th Century-Fox. Sherry started as a math teacher, and then turned to actress, to script girl, to producer, to studio president.

Age: 43
Weight at 21: 135 pounds
Weight today: 133 pounds

BREAKFAST

Sherry is careful never to skip breakfast, and she consumes the same breakfast every day: orange juice; oatmeal or a low-fat, low-sugar cold cereal; and a bran muffin. She doesn't drink coffee.

LUNCH

Sherry eats lunch from two basic recipes: chicken salad or fish, each with a glass of Perrier.

DINNER

Sherry has a salad and most of the time, either fish, chicken, or pasta. She doesn't eat red meat and doesn't drink any hard alcohol, but has a glass of wine with dinner and, once in a while, dessert.

EXERCISE

Sherry plays tennis four days a week for one hour.

COMMENTS

As a motion picture producer, Sherry is often on location. On one of her recent pictures she was in Vancouver, where she spent six months rising at 6:00 A.M. and getting back to the hotel about 10:00 P.M. This makes it tough to stick with her eating habits, but she stays as close to her basic recipes as possible.

The toughest part of location work for Sherry is the difficulty of getting regular exercise. If she has to go a few days without any workouts, she gets irritable and has to watch her temper. When that happens, Sherry makes time to go for a long walk or a light jog.

After six months in Vancouver, Sherry's weight had crept up to 140 pounds. By returning to her regular eating and exercise habits, she quickly got back to 133.

◄ ◄ 13 ► ►

How to Make New (Good) Habits Become Old (Good) Habits

No More Excuses

In Chapter 14 I will show you step-by-step how to start *The 7-Week Victory Diet*. We'll do it one week at a time, adopting one new habit each week. At the end of seven weeks you'll be eating from only eleven basic recipes, and the 11-in-7 Plan will start to become part of your daily habits. Once you are fully used to these new (good) habits, once they become comfortable old (good) habits, you'll be set. You will be lean and healthy, full of vitality and energy.

Before I show you how easy it is to begin this plan, though, I want to clear the closet of all those excuses you've been using to rationalize why you can't lose weight. I may sound a little rough-handed just laying them out on the table, but that's the best way I know to get you to realize they are all cop-outs!

With no apologies, then, here's the list:

1. Claiming you can't lose weight because you have glandular problems is a cop-out. Less than 3 percent of the population suffer from thyroid problems, and those who do can receive effective control of their glandular imbalance through proper medication.

2. Claiming you can't lose weight because you're genetically encoded to be fat is a cop-out. It's true that some people have body shapes more prone to gaining weight than others, but body shape doesn't mean you have to be overweight. Maybe you're not perfect. Maybe you don't have a Jane Fonda figure or maybe Arnold Schwarzenegger got your share of muscles when they were passed out. Don't worry, because nobody's dealt a perfect hand. *The trick is to decide you're going to play the best game possible with the cards you're holding. Once you decide that, you'll discover you've got more going for you than you ever imagined.*

3. Claiming you can't lose weight because you're older and your metabolism has slowed is a cop-out. You may have a slower metabolism, but you *can* change it. The right eating habits with the right exercise habits will get your metabolism up and your weight down.

4. Claiming you can't lose weight because you don't have time to follow complicated dieting plans is a cop-out because with *The 7-Week Victory Diet*, there are no complicated recipes. This plan is designed for people who don't have time to be fat.

So decide right now that you have no more excuses. Decide right now that you are going to begin *The 7-Week Victory Diet*.

Make a commitment, then make a commitment to keep the commitment. Get positive and you'll get thin.

Set Your Starting Line

Any time you set a goal for yourself, it's much easier to attain it if you set up signposts to measure your progress. Learning to change your eating and exercise habits is no different. The more measurements you have to register your progress toward winning the food and fitness fight, the more encouragement you'll have to stick to your new habits.

Here are a number of measurements to consider recording before you start on the Victory Diet. These measurements will be your starting line in tracking your progress.

Pulse Rate

Your pulse rate is easy to measure, and you should get in the habit of keeping tabs on it. There are two easy ways to measure your pulse. The first is to place your index finger on your carotid artery. This is in your neck, tucked under the crook in your jawbone. Explore the area with your finger until you feel your blood beating through, then count the number of beats. I usually count the number of beats in fifteen seconds, then multiply by four.

The second method is to measure your pulse on the inside of your wrist. Again, use your index finger and place it on your wrist about an inch below your lower thumb joint, pressing it around until you pick up your pulse.

Your resting pulse should be taken immediately after you wake up and before you get out of bed in the morning. The average resting heart rate is between sixty and eighty beats per minute for men and between seventy and ninety for women.

You should also take your pulse three times while you are exercising: once at the end of your warm-up, again at the end of the aerobic part of your workout, and once more when you have finished exercising and have completed your cool-down stretches.

Keep track of your pulse throughout the day. As you exercise more, you'll find that your resting pulse will decrease, and you'll recover your normal pulse more quickly after you exercise. Tracking your decreasing pulse rate should be your incentive, your "carrot on a stick," encouraging you to keep up your exercise habits.

Body Fat

In Chapter 9 (pages 105–109) we discussed why measuring your body fat is the most illuminating way of measuring your body weight. If you haven't read that section, you should return to it now, before you go any further.

This is an important part of your starting line measurements. After you've been on the Victory Diet about seven weeks, go back and have your body fat measured again. The difference should be all the encouragement you need to stick with your new eating and exercise habits.

Blood Test

Regardless of your age, it's a good idea to get a blood test before you start *The 7-Week Victory Diet* so that you know your cholesterol, HDL, and triglyceride levels (see "How to Read Your Own Blood Test" on pages 169–171. These are important measurements of your starting line.

To get a blood analysis, go to a health clinic or, if there's one in your area, a blood analysis center. There's some controversy surrounding these latest entrepreneurial health services that are starting to appear in shopping centers around the country. They are staffed with trained technicians who take a blood sample and then either send you a report of the analysis or explain the various readings to you. Doctors who are critical of this new service argue that blood analysis alone isn't a complete measure of your physical well-being and that it may mislead people into thinking they are healthy when they are not.

This may be so, but when used in conjunction with regular medical checkups, these centers are a convenient place where you can keep track of your own blood chemistry and see for yourself the progress you're making with your new eating and exercise habits.

How to Read Your Own Blood Test

When you get the results back from your blood analysis, don't be intimidated by all the numbers and abbreviations. There should be someone at the clinic where your blood sample was collected who can help you interpret the results, but as with other areas of medicine and nutrition, I strongly suggest that you teach yourself the basics.

Of the 20 to 30 measurements likely to appear on your analysis, there are 5 with regard to nutrition that you really need to know about.

1. *Cholesterol*. Many doctors won't sound a warning until your cholesterol level gets to 240. That's dangerous. If your cholesterol is over 200, you should be alarmed. If it's over 200 and your HDL level is under 30 (mg/dl),

(continued)

you should be doubly alarmed. In fact, you should seek the advice of a knowledgeable doctor.

2. *HDL*. The "good" cholesterol, HDL is the agent that acts to remove cholesterol from your arterial walls and flush it out of your system. You want your HDL level to be 40 (mg/dl) or higher.

3. *Triglycerides*. This number indicates the amount of fat in your blood and tells you a lot about your diet. Eating fats and sugars raises the triglyceride level, and eating complex carbohydrates lowers it.

If your triglyceride level is over 140, you should consider altering your diet. Make a reading of 100 or lower your target.

4. *Uric Acid*. This is usually the culprit that causes gout. If your blood analysis shows high levels of uric acid, this may explain problems you may have with arthritis or aching joints. By following the low-fat, high-complex carbohydrate diet in *Win the Food Fight*, you'll find that your uric acid level will drop. Your goal should be a level of 5 mg/dl or less for women, and 6 mg/dl or less for men.

Be aware, however, that sudden changes in eating habits can cause a temporary rise in uric acid levels, even if your new habits are good ones. The reason: Uric acid is manufactured from compounds called purines, and when you change your eating habits to foods low in purines, your body makes up for it by releasing the uric acid stored in your tissues. If you have a high uric acid level shortly after starting new eating habits, don't despair. Give it a month, and get another blood analysis. By then your uric acid level should have dropped.

5. *Glucose*. Since glucose measures your blood sugar level when you've been fasting, get your blood analysis done in the morning, before eating anything. Too little sugar in your blood means you don't have sufficient energy available for both exercise and thinking (remember, the brain works on glucose!). Too much sugar, though, and you could be a candidate for diabetes.

If you follow the right balance of proteins, carbohydrates, and fats in your eating habits, and if you get a few minutes of low-volume exercise every day, you shouldn't have any problems keeping the right glucose levels—a reading between 85 and 100 mg/dl.

Blood Pressure

High blood pressure—hypertension—has been positively linked to a rogue's gallery of potentially fatal diseases: stroke, heart attack, and kidney failure.

High blood pressure has also been positively linked with bad diet and a lack of exercise. Conversely, it's been proven positively that a good diet and regular exercise lower blood pressure. That's why knowing your blood pressure is an important part of your starting-line measurements.

Blood pressure is usually the first measurement taken when you go to the doctor's office.

The problem with spot checking blood pressure is that it fluctuates so much. If you've had a stressful day, or if someone nearly ran into you on the way to the doctor's office, chances are your blood pressure will be high.

That's why I recommend getting your own machine and taking your blood pressure once a week. There are now on the market several models of blood pressure gauges designed for home use, and most of them are moderately priced.

It's Best to Know Your Starting-Line Statistics . . . But Don't Let That Stop You from Starting

Your starting-line statistics consist of your pulse rate, percentage of body fat, blood cholesterol and other key blood-chemistry figures, and blood pressure. If you get these measurements as you start *The 7-Week Victory Diet*, and follow up with a second set of measurements seven weeks later, you'll have graphic proof that your new eating and exercise habits work.

You do not *have* to know your starting-line measurements in order to begin *The 7-Week Victory Diet*. This plan is designed around the fact that you are a busy person and can't afford the time to follow a complicated diet and exercise program. Knowing your starting-line measurements makes it easier to change your eating and exercise habits because it gives you supportive feedback. The measurements, however, have nothing to do with how well the plan works. You are going to lose body fat and lower your cholesterol level, your blood pressure, and your pulse—whether or not you know the figures.

So if you are too busy to get your body fat measured or to have a blood test, don't use it as an excuse to postpone beginning this plan. You may have more fun if you do know your starting-line measurements, but it's much better to give your health the benefits of these new habits even if you don't know the quantitative results. Just rest assured that those results will come.

You Don't Need Willpower

Most people think starting a diet plan requires gut-grinding, teeth-gnashing, eye-popping willpower. With *Win the Food Fight*, nothing could be further from the truth.

With this plan, you don't need willpower. All you need is intention. There's a big difference between the two. *Willpower* implies a struggle with yourself. Your instincts want you to do one thing while your intellect struggles to do another. *Intention*, on the other hand, implies that you have a planned purpose. It means you have focused on a goal and have come up with a method of achieving it.

I want to help you achieve the right intention. By the time you finish this section, you will have a goal in mind: to lose weight, lower your cholesterol, and lower your blood pressure. In short, to get trim, fit, and healthy. You will also realize you need no willpower to achieve this goal. Why?

Because you will be changing your eating and exercise habits in increments, a little at a time. You'll never be asked to change your habits in any single step big enough to be uncomfortable.

If someone is overweight and out of shape, and if they've been that way a good portion of their adult life, you simply can't ask them to go cold turkey on a Spartan diet plan. No one has or should be expected to have that kind of willpower. Losing weight and keeping it off has nothing to do with starving, denial, and misery. Any diet or exercise plan built around any of those three oppressors is doomed to failure.

The easiest way to change your habits is in increments. That's why *The 7-Week Victory Diet* is broken down into weekly segments. Each week you make one small change in your eating or exercise habits, and you get used to it for the next six days before you make the next incremental change.

Change and habits. It's really as easy as that.

Ann Hand

Well-known Washington hostess, Ann is also the wife of the former chief of protocol of the United States.

Age: 54
Weight at 21: 120 pounds
Weight today: 115 pounds

BREAKFAST

Six days a week Ann has a slice of cantaloupe or a few strawberries or half a grapefruit and a bowl of Shredded Wheat. On Sundays Ann has French toast made as follows: Low-Cal bread (40 calories per slice) dipped in one egg (100 calories), and cooked lightly in a frying pan sprayed with Pam, served with two table-spoons of Low-Cal syrup for a total of roughly 200 calories.

LUNCH

Ann has tuna or fruit salad for lunch.

DINNER

Seven days a week Ann eats exactly the same thing for dinner: fish with a baked potato and vegetable, such as broccoli or cauliflower, and an occasional glass of wine. Absolutely no red meat and no dessert.

COMMENTS

As wife of former ambassador and U.S. chief of protocol Lloyd Hand, Ann is extremely active in Washington's diplomatic and social life, and she is often out six nights a week. For most of her adult life—before she adopted her present eating and exercise habits—her weight was 145 pounds. For 30 years she tried diet centers, diet pills, shots, and other stop-gap measures. Then a year ago she decided to remodel her eating habits as she might remodel her home.

With her low-fat, high-complex carbohydrate diet, Ann quickly lost weight. She adopted a low-volume exercise program that included walking and swimming. Even though she and her husband are out nearly every evening, Ann always eats dinner at 6:00 P.M. and just nibbles at her food later in the evening.

For the past year, Ann has maintained her weight at 115 pounds. She never feels hungry, and she is so comfortable with her new habits that she can't imagine ever changing.

◄ ◄ 14 ► ►

The 11-in-7 Strategy: Seven Weeks to Eleven Basic Menus

Most of us eat from only a few basic recipes. And I've showed you that to lose weight permanently all you need to do is change a handful of your old bad habits for a handful of good ones. I took a close look at these good habits: the Victory Breakfast, Lunch, and Dinner menus, and the Victory program of low-volume and high-volume exercises.

In other words, I've given you all the ammunition you need to take aim at your weight problem. Here then is the easy step-by-step program you will follow to win the food fight—to change your eating and exercise habits in only seven weeks.

Seven Weeks to Winning
the Food Fight

Caution: Make certain you adopt these new habits one week at a time. Don't do anything in addition to what is recommended for each week. The way to make new habits become comfortable old habits is to acquire them gradually.

WEEK 1

Old habit: Eating the wrong breakfast.
Focus on: Eating the oatmeal Victory Breakfast five days a week.

WEEK 2

Old habit: Eating too much salt.
                Drinking too little water.
Focus on: Eliminating all salty foods and drinking five glasses of water a day.

WEEK 3

Old habit: Lack of exercise.
Focus on: Beginning each day with ten minutes of low-volume exercise.

WEEK 4

Old habit: Eating dinner too late.
Focus on: Eating dinner three hours before going to bed.

WEEK 5

Old habit: Eating too much sugar.
            Drinking too much alcohol.
Focus on: Eliminating sodas, packaged food, and other sources of refined sugar and eliminating or reducing alcohol.

WEEK 6

Old habit: Eating the wrong lunch.
Focus on: Eating from any of the four Victory Lunch menus.

WEEK 7

Old habit: Eating the wrong dinner.
Focus on: Eating from any of the five Victory Dinner menus.

That's it—seven easy weeks to victory in the food fight. Now let's take a close-up look at each week.

Close-Up on Week 1

New Habit: Eat the Oatmeal Victory Breakfast at Least Five Days a Week

Since you probably already eat the same thing for breakfast every day, this first step is easy. All you have to do is replace whatever you now eat for breakfast with the Oatmeal Victory Breakfast outlined in Chapter 4.

This is the single most important new habit you will acquire on *The 7-Week Victory Diet*, and that's why it's the first habit I ask you to embrace. The Oatmeal Victory Breakfast will increase the fiber in your diet, causing the rest of the food you eat in the day to pass quickly through your system so you don't gain weight. Eating a big breakfast will also pattern the rest of your day's meals, keeping you from overeating at lunch and dinner.

After you've been on the Victory Plan for seven weeks you can occasionally substitute the oatmeal breakfast menu with the cold-cereal menu. But to start, you need to get in the oatmeal habit. And you must be sure to prepare your oatmeal using skim milk, with no added sugar or salt. This will help accustom your taste buds to the other new eating habits you will start on Week 2.

Close-Up on Week 2

New Habit: Eat Less Salt and Drink More Water

Making your oatmeal without salt will set you up for the second week of *Winning the Food Fight*. The less salt you eat, the less taste you'll have for it. Here are a few tips on how to start reducing the amount of salt you eat:

- Take the salt shaker off your dining or breakfast table. You can even throw it away (as long as it's not your late aunt's cut crystal).

- Stop eating salted snack foods. This may seem a little harsh, but if you substitute fruit or applesauce as a snack (following the snack plan in Chapter 8), it won't take many days before you'll wince if you get too close to a potato chip: The salt and grease will taste like brine sludge.

- Stop adding salt to boiling water to cook oatmeal, pasta, rice, and the like. Do not add salt to any of your food.

The second change in Week 2 is to begin drinking five glasses of water a day. Start by drinking a glass of warm lemon water first thing when you get up. Drink a second glass in the midmorning, a third glass midafternoon, a fourth glass one hour before dinner, and a fifth glass one hour before bedtime.

Close-Up on Week 3

New Habit: Low-Volume Exercises

You'll find getting used to the low-volume exercises outlined in Chapter 10 is easy because they are quick and enjoyable. All you have to do is budget ten extra minutes in the morning, starting at the beginning of the third week.

I'm not going to ask you to adopt any high-volume habits at this time. Save those for later, after you've gotten used to your new eating habits and your low-volume exercise habits. As you begin to get in shape from the low-volume exercises, you will naturally want to step up the pace. Your body will tell you when it wants to start a high-volume program.

Close-Up on Week 4

New Habit: Eat Dinner at Least Three Hours Before Going to Bed

Of all the habits I'm asking you to adopt, I realize this may be the most difficult. That's why you have to decide here and now to make the necessary changes in your daily schedule to adopt this new eating habit. This is one of the most important parts in the battle for permanent weight loss. *When* you eat is as important as *what* you eat. If you have made the commitment to lose weight, then you can also make up your mind to do what you need to do so that you can eat dinner at least three hours before retiring.

Turn back to Chapter 7 and take another look at the tips I give you on how to eat dinner as early as possible, and then decide to do it!

Close-Up on Week 5

New Habit: Eliminate Refined Sugar and Reduce Alcohol

Sugar calories are empty calories. They have no nutrients —no vitamins, minerals, or fiber—and they cause an insulin reaction that lowers your blood sugar level. This in turn can make you irritable.

During Week 5, stop adding refined sugar to your food. If you use it in your coffee or tea, try substituting a small amount of honey (the sugar in honey is no better for you than other types, but because its taste is stronger, you can use less). You can also substitute Equal. As previously mentioned, it's better not to use any sweetener. Some people, however, just can't handle cold-turkey sugar shutoff. If that's the case, Equal seems to be the best product on the market at this time. But, if you can, stop adding sugar to your breakfast cereal. For the first few days you may find this odd, but your taste buds will quickly adapt and after a while you will actually prefer the flavor. Instead, try raisins. They are naturally sweet and full of iron.

Also during Week 5, cut out soft drinks (including sugar-free diet drinks). Instead, try a blend of 50 percent soda or mineral water and 50 percent juice such as apple, cranberry, or white grape.

This week also concentrate on cutting down on packaged foods that contain lots of sugar. Get in the habit of reading labels. If you want a sweet snack, eat a piece of fruit.

This is the week to start reducing the amount of alcohol you drink or, better still, give it up altogether. Remember, alcohol is just like sugar: All you get is triglycerides and empty calories devoid of nutrition. In fact, alcohol actually drains your system of vitamins such as B–12, niacin, and thiamine. Alcohol makes you fat. Gram for gram, it has almost twice as many calories as protein or carbohydrates. I had one friend who felt he was a little overweight and who had an average of two or three drinks a day. He cut this back to one short drink every other day and lost eight pounds *without any other changes in his diet*.

The first two weeks of *The 7-Week Victory Diet* maintain your alcohol consumption at no more than one drink a day. If you take another look at the Winner's Circle profiles, you'll find that most limit themselves to a single glass of wine with dinner.

Close-Up on Week 6

New Habit: Eat the Victory Lunch

This week will be easy. Since there's a good chance you already eat from a few basic lunch recipes, all you have to do is replace what you're now eating with the four basic lunch menus outlined in Chapter 6. Start eating from these easy-to-follow menus five days a week.

You'll be following the Victory Breakfast and Lunch—both designed to reduce the overall fat in your diet. As a result, you'll find your taste buds changing. You'll get used to the clean taste of a fat-reduced diet. This will make it much easier to move to the final week of the 11-in-7 Victory Plan.

Close-Up on Week 7

New Habit: Eating from the Victory Dinner Menus

The final step to adopting the complete Victory Diet is to start eating from the five basic dinner menus outlined in Chapter 7 at least five days a week. Following these simple menus will significantly increase the amount of complex carbohydrates you eat and reduce the amount of fat in your diet.

It's Really That Simple

Changing your habits is like acquiring a taste for a new food. The new habits—the new "taste"—may seem strange until you get used to it, but after a while you'll be hooked, and you'll never want to go back to your old ways. Remember, when you've successfully changed your habits, when they have become time-tested old habits that have served you well in the battle against overeating and being overweight, you won't want to deviate from them. You also will have changed the way you think about yourself. You will feel better about life in general because you will have put yourself in charge of your body instead of allowing yourself to be controlled by food. You will have won the food fight. This simple fact will inspire confidence that will carry over to everything else you do.

You will be at the helm, steering the course and shape not only of your body but also of your entire life.

No more excuses. Go for it.

Clint Eastwood

Clint has had a long and immensely successful acting career, and has added directing (and serving as mayor of Carmel, California) to his very impressive list of credits.

Age: 58
Weight at 21: 198
Weight today: 203

BREAKFAST

Every morning Clint eats a bowl of oatmeal or oat bran with a fruit plate and yogurt. He doesn't drink coffee.

LUNCH

Clint's lunch is a bit unusual. He eats sushi seven days a week. Although some of us might find it difficult to find a sushi bar every day at noon, it certainly fits the protein-at-lunch part of *The 7-Week Victory Diet*.

DINNER

Each evening Clint eats either fish or pasta, and a salad. Occasionally he substitutes chicken for the fish. He never eats red meat. He has wine or an occasional beer with dinner.

EXERCISE

Clint works out forty-five minutes a day, combining lifting weights with general exercise and jogging.

COMMENTS

When he's shooting a film, Clint says it's very difficult to maintain his usual eating and exercise habits because of the extremely long working days. On location, his weight may sneak up to 210. However, as soon as the film wraps, he immediately returns to his regular eating habits and quickly reaches his target weight.

Clint does like to have a couple of beers on weekends with his pals but, despite his heavy schedule, he stays in great shape. He is very active in sports, including snow skiing, waterskiing, and bodysurfing. Looking good and maintaining his health are, of course, important to his career, but even if he never made another movie, there is no doubt Clint would maintain his eating and exercise habits throughout his life.

◄ Part V ►

Maintenance: Staying in the Winner's Circle Once You Reach Your Target Weight

How to Stay in the Winner's Circle

You've reached your target weight. You're used to eating from the eleven Victory Menus. Your new (good) habits have become old (good) habits. Can you continue to eat from your eleven basic menus for the rest of your life?

Of course not. Even though you are comfortable with your new habits, at some point you will feel that you want something different. At some point you'll hear about a new recipe that sounds good, you'll have a new dish at a friend's house that you enjoy, or a good meal at a restaurant that you want to try to prepare yourself.

But how do you accommodate this change and still stay within the Victory Diet? How can you be certain that you will stay at your target weight—that you'll stay in the Winner's Circle?

The answer is that you have to know enough about the difference between what is good for you and what is bad in order to judge whether the new recipe, or the new food, fits within the Victory Diet. But don't panic. It's really not difficult to learn enough to easily stay in the Winner's Circle.

The Winner's Circle of Food

What constitutes the Winner's Circle of food? It's a combination of foods that the U.S. Surgeon General and other medical groups such as the American Heart Association have found ideal in maintaining a healthy, balanced diet. If we break down these foods into a chart, they look like this:

Food Classification	Percentage of Total Daily Calories
Protein	12
Fat	28
Carbohydrates	60*

*It's important that most of the carbohydrates you eat be complex carbohydrates and not simple sugars. Eating complex carbohydrates will ensure that you get the fiber you need each day.

But how is a chart like this useful in figuring out your daily eating habits? How do you tell if your day's meals contain 28 percent fat or less? Obviously you don't want to carry a food chart and calculator everywhere you go. If you're like me, you don't even want to think about trying to break down foods into proteins, fats, and carbohydrates.

The good news is that you don't have to perform a lot of calorie calculations in order to stay within the Winner's Circle. Once you learn a few basics about the kinds of foods that are good for you and the kinds that are bad, you can stay within the Winner's Circle without even thinking.

And after reading this much of the book, you already know the kinds of foods that are good for you. You know you need a whole-grain cereal low in fat and salt each day for breakfast. You know that oatmeal is the best cereal for you but that you can select others if they contain little or no sugar, salt, or added fat.

You know that fish and chicken are the best sources of protein because they are lower in fat than is red meat. Turkey, rabbit, and many wild game meats are also good, however.

You know that a fiber-rich starch staple should be included in your dinner meal as often as possible, and that whole-grain brown rice or potatoes are hard to beat. You can enjoy other grains, too, such as barley or corn on the cob. If you feel like an eating adventure, there are more exotic grains such as bulgur, couscous, kasha, and quinoa. All types of beans are fantastic, and don't forget lentils, which are very fast cooking.

You know that the vegetables called *Cruciferae,* such as broccoli and cauliflower, are fantastic sources of vitamins and fiber. You'll stay within the Winner's Circle with just about any raw or lightly steamed vegetable that suits your fancy—red and green peppers, brussels sprouts, kale, carrots, spinach, eggplant, tomatoes—the choice is endless.

Staying with these types of wholesome foods, you can design your own repertoire of favorite meals, just as the celebrities in our Winner's Circle Profiles have done. You will still find it easier to keep the number of meals to a dozen or so, and, if you are like most people, you'll find yourself doing this anyway. Remember, the average American eats from about a dozen basic recipes, and the secret of the Victory Diet is to make those menus healthy ones.

You've reached your target weight—you're in the Winner's Circle. You know the kind of foods that can keep you in that circle. To stay there, it helps to know why those foods are good for you and why other foods are bad. That's why I want to spend the next two sections discussing the worst culprits in the Standard American Diet: fat and sugar.

The Winner's Circle of Food

Fresh fruits: grapefruit, oranges, lemons, peaches, pears, plums, cantaloupe, apples, grapes, strawberries, blueberries, kiwifruit, apricots, figs, bananas, raisins, papayas, watermelon, honeydew, limes, cherries

Whole-grain cereals and breads: oatmeal, oat bran, pasta, rice, wheat, barley, corn, kasha, popcorn, couscous, bulgur, quinoa, rye

Fresh vegetables: avocados, lima beans, green beans, snow peas, beets, cabbage, broccoli, brussels sprouts, potatoes, green peppers, red peppers, carrots, cauliflower, celery, chard, onions, artichokes, kale, leeks, lettuce, spinach, mushrooms, okra, parsley, parsnips, peas, pumpkin, radishes, rhubarb, turnips, bok choy, zucchini, tomatoes, acorn squash, butternut squash, sweet potatoes, eggplants, watercress, jicama, green onions

Lean poultry and fish: chicken, turkey, salmon, halibut, mackerel, trout, swordfish, tuna, pickerel, cod, flounder, snapper, grouper, wild game

Dried beans: lima, black, kidney, garbanzo, great northern, navy, pinto, soy, lentil, split pea

Very-low- or non-fat dairy products: skim milk, low- or non-fat yogurt, very-low- or non-fat cottage cheese, hoop cheese, string cheese

The American Diet Is Fat with Fat

If you're an average American, the amount of fat you eat is between 40 and 50 percent of all the calories you take in! Just imagine: About half the food you eat deposits readily around your waist to make you sluggish instead of burning efficiently in your muscles to make you full of energy. *Overconsumption of fat is the single biggest cause of obesity in America.*

It's also the single biggest cause of diet-related disease and illness. A high-fat diet greatly increases the risk of heart attack, stroke, colon cancer, and diabetes. That's one of the big reasons *The 7-Week Victory Diet* is designed around eleven habit-forming good menus. And that is why, once you reach your target weight and have the option of designing your own menus, you must make sure to keep the fat content of your meals to a minimum.

If you still don't think this is important, here are a few facts that should turn you around:

- One study showed that within an hour of eating a high-fat meal, blood cells actually begin to stick together, making the flow of blood sludgelike. Continued high-fat consumption may eventually lead to a stroke.

- Several major studies, including the long-running Framingham (Massachusetts) study, have indicated that a high-fat diet increases the risk of cancer of the colon by 70 percent and more.

- Researchers have shown that a high-fat diet blocks the proper functioning of insulin. Reducing dietary fat can relieve the need for insulin therapy in up to 75 percent of those who have suffered diabetes as adults.

- A recent study showed that for every 1 percent rise in a person's cholesterol level (and cholesterol level is directly related to consumption of fat), there is a 2 percent rise in risk of heart disease. And heart disease is the biggest killer in the United States, claiming nearly twice as many lives annually as all forms of cancer combined.

Cholesterol: A Subject Close to Your Heart

Cholesterol is essential to your body's ability to build cell membranes. Your body also has the ability to manufacture all the cholesterol it needs to function properly. The extra cholesterol you get from your diet is what does you harm.

Scientists now believe that your body differentiates between the cholesterol it makes itself and that which it gets from your diet. Dietary cholesterol is much more likely to end up in your blood where it collects on your arterial walls to form deposits called *plaque*. Enough plaque can restrict the free flow of blood to your heart, resulting in a heart attack.

What you need to accomplish is to reduce the amount of cholesterol in your diet. What you need to remember is that cholesterol is found only in animal products. In other words, the only way you can get extra cholesterol in your diet is by eating high-fat meats, eggs, or high-fat dairy products. That's why on the Victory Diet it's essential for you to design menus that keep these three culprits to a minimum.

That's not the full story, however. You also should design menus that avoid saturated fats and saturated or hydrogenated oils. Why? Because even though some saturated oils (such as the palm kernel oil and coconut oil used commonly in packaged cookies, crackers, and snack foods) may be free of cholesterol, they can nevertheless raise your cholesterol level by raising the amount of low-density lipoprotein (LDL) in your blood. Because

"Don't Worry, Your Cholesterol Is Only 240."

Finally doctors seem to be joining the war against cholesterol but, as usual, they're a day late and a dollar short. A recent article in the *Wall Street Journal* states, "If tests confirm the [cholesterol] level is above 200 but less than 240 or 250, the doctor will *probably* (emphasis mine) urge the patient to go on a low-fat diet."

It reminds me of how long it took doctors and the AMA to come out against smoking. Another authority in this article is quoted as saying that a 10 percent drop in the average cholesterol level of Americans could reduce the number of annual deaths from heart attack in the United States from 540,000 to maybe 440,000.

Why should more than 400,000 deaths be acceptable? Why can't more doctors realize that a cholesterol level of 200 to 240 is unacceptable? Why can't more doctors learn the basics of good nutrition, so that they can prescribe healthy, low-fat diets combined with easy-to-follow exercise programs for anybody with a cholesterol level above 200?

I suspect that the medical profession will eventually come around but probably at a glacial pace. My advice: Don't wait. Take action yourself. Get a blood test. Analyze it yourself. And then follow *The 7-Week Victory Diet*.

cholesterol is not water-soluble, it relies on this LDL to hitch a ride through your blood where it can then deposit on your arterial walls.

Eating from menus that are laden with saturated fat such as coconut or palm oil therefore increases the harmful deposits of cholesterol in your arteries even though the coconut or palm oil is a plant product and therefore has no actual cholesterol in it. It's important, then, to know how to avoid these harmful oils. That's why in the next chapter I will show you how to shop for foods that are free of these culprits.

Fat may be the biggest single reason America is overweight, but it's not the only reason. The other major culprit is sugar.

How to Eat 120 Pounds of Sugar

Let's imagine that one morning there's a knock on your door. You're surprised to find a burly teamster-type standing in your doorway with a big sack slung over his shoulder. He reads your name on his delivery order.

"Yes, that's me.

"I got something for ya," he says.

"What is it?"

"Sugar. Sixty pounds. Wait right here. I got one more sack in the truck."

He comes back in a minute with the other sack. It's the same size.

"Okay, bub, sign here."

"What am I supposed to do with this?"

"Eat it!"

"Eat it?"

"My orders here say you gotta eat it and you got one year to do it. I'll be back in twelve months with another load, so I wanna see this stuff gone by then. Got it?"

You pull the two huge sacks into your kitchen and sigh. One hundred twenty pounds of sugar! How can you eat all of it, even if you do have a year?

Well, surprise.

If you're on the Standard American Diet (S.A.D.), you already are eating it. It's in almost every item of processed food you buy: soft drinks, cookies, ice cream, white bread. There's a teaspoon of it in every tablespoon of ketchup you eat. It all adds up to 120 pounds a year. Enough to strain the back of a burly teamster.

My anecdote about the teamster may be fanciful, but the facts are not: For the average American, sugar makes up nearly 25 percent of his or her total calories consumed.

That's a lot of sugar—and a lot of calories, too, calories that are devoid of any of the forty-four nutrients we humans need to maintain good health.

In other words, sugar calories are empty calories. Sugar takes the place of the food you *should* be eating, such as complex carbohydrates, that *would* supply you with vitamins, minerals, and fiber—as well as the calories you need for energy. And the calories from complex carbohydrates are slow burning, giving you longer-lasting energy. Sugar, in contrast, is a false pick-me-up: You get an initial boost of energy only to be let down shortly thereafter.

Most of you have experienced the personality-altering consequences of eating too much sugar. What actually happens is that sugar raises your blood's glucose level, which triggers the release of insulin, the hormone that enables the glucose to be burned by your body. The trouble is that in some people the sugar causes too much insulin to be released, using up too much glucose, which can lead to low blood sugar, or hypoglycemia. This in turn leaves you irritable and moody.

Sugar leaves you hungry. Eating too much sugar can then lead to further overeating.

The extra insulin in your blood caused by eating refined

sugar also causes your body to store as fat more of the other food you eat. All of which means eating sugar tends to put the pounds on, even beyond the actual calories from the sugar itself.

I'm not saying you should give up sugar completely. I am saying you should design your menus around natural foods that keep sugar to a naturally low level. You'll find that once you do start to wean yourself from sugar your craving for sweets will diminish. In fact, the thought of anything on the order of chocolate fudge cake will make your toes curl.

It's Good to Be Allergic to C.A.T.S.

C.A.T.S. is an acronym my kids use for caffeine, alcohol, tobacco, and salt—four culprits you need to know about so you know why to avoid them.

Caffeine

Whether or not caffeine is bad for you has been the subject of considerable debate. A study recently completed by Johns Hopkins University found that people who drink six or more cups of coffee a day have an increased rate of heart disease. The reason is that high amounts of caffeine can cause up to a 14 percent increase in your cholesterol level.

Caffeine is addictive, and too much of it raises your pulse rate, makes your heart beat irregularly, makes you irritable and jumpy, and can give you insomnia, diarrhea, and even nausea.

Small amounts of caffeine, though, don't seem to have any measurably bad effects. Even though I think it's better to give the stuff up, a single cup of tea or coffee in the morning shouldn't harm you. Just try to keep your total daily intake of caffeine to 100 milligrams or less. Here's a chart that will help you know what that means in practical terms:

Coffee, "dripolated"	146 mg per cup
Coffee, percolated	110 mg per cup
Coffee, instant	66 mg per cup
Teabag, five-minute brew	46 mg per cup
Teabag, one-minute brew	28 mg per cup
Coca-Cola	65 mg per 12-oz can
Diet Dr. Pepper	54 mg per 12-oz can
Pepsi-Cola	43 mg per 12-oz can
Excedrin	64 mg per tablet
Anacin	32 mg per tablet

The safest strategy is to avoid coffee as much as possible. That doesn't mean you have to give up the enjoyment of wrapping your fingers around a hot mug on a cold morning. Try these coffee substitutes:

1. *Postum*. This is a roasted barley powder that has realistic coffee taste. With some heated skim milk, it's as good as *café au lait*.
2. *Celestial Seasoning's Roastaroma*. This winner is the famous herbal tea company's answer to a no-caffeine, coffee-like beverage.
3. *Bigelow's "Take-a-Break" Herbal Tea*. This no-caffeine roasted-barley and spice tea is a great coffee substitute.

Alcohol

As with caffeine, there's a lot of controversy over whether the effects of drinking alcohol in small amounts are good, bad, or indifferent. One thing is certain: Even a moderate amount of alcohol can put pounds around you. I've had friends who have made only one change in their dietary habits—to stop drinking —and who lost ten pounds in a matter of days or weeks.

Beyond that, studies trying to measure the health effects of alcohol have reached mixed conclusions. Some recent reports have noted that many wines and liquors contain high levels of urethane, a known carcinogen.

In balance, it seems that an occasional glass of wine or a bottle of beer can do you little harm. More than a glass a day, though, and you're going to start gaining weight.

Tobacco

So much has been written about the cancer hazards of smoking that it would be pointless to discuss it here. I'll simply say that if you smoke, you're asking for trouble. If you need help to stop, consult one of the many books on the subject, or enroll in one of the behavior-modification clinics around the country designed to assist people in breaking this worst of all habits.

Salt

It's been estimated that eating the Standard American Diet gives you between twenty and thirty times the amount of salt you need to remain healthy. It's also been estimated that one in six Americans develops high blood pressure as a result.

A high-salt diet has also been implicated in stomach cancer. The Japanese, who as a nation have an extremely high salt intake in their diet (an average of 7½ teaspoons a day!), have the highest rate of stomach cancer in the world. It's been shown that excessive salt actually eats away the stomach lining.

Salt is essential to our body's chemical balance. In past civilizations where salt was scarce, it was highly prized. Roman soldiers were paid in part with salt, and that's actually the origin of the word "salary." Our bodies need only fifty milligrams a day, and the average American eats up to five grams a day. That's more than two teaspoons of salt.

Salt, which is used to enhance flavor and as a preservative, is one of the principal hazards of eating prepared and packaged foods. It's in practically everything. A can of soup, for example, can have up to 1,000 milligrams of salt. A serving of Wheaties contains 370 milligrams (although the manufacturer says they are going to change this). A Big Mac with fries adds up to about 1,400 milligrams!

To reduce salt in your diet, then, you have to reduce the amount of packaged food you eat, and you have to learn to read labels. And you have to be careful what you order when you eat out. You also need to get out of the habit of adding extra salt to food. You would be wise to decide that you're never going to touch a salt shaker again. You simply don't need it. As with other things that you begin to eliminate from your diet, once you start reducing the amount of salt, you'll lose a taste for it. Food low in salt will not taste bland. In fact, salted food that in the past may have tasted normal to you will seem like brine.

There are other things you can add to your food as salt substitutes:

HERBS *(single or mixed)*   **SPICES**

Marjoram   Cumin
Dill   Chili powder
Oregano   Curry
Basil
Rosemary
Thyme

OTHER

Spike
Bragg Sauce
Lemon juice
Lime juice

Animal fats, saturated fats, hydrogenated oils, sugars, C.A.T.S.—those are the bad guys to avoid when designing your

Victory Menus. In the next chapter, I'll provide a few shopping and cooking tips to help you steer clear of these culprits.

Richard and Lili Zanuck

Lili Zanuck

Motion picture producer Lili's first venture with her husband, Dick, was the highly acclaimed and hugely popular movie *Cocoon*. Dick and Lili are a very successful husband-and-wife producing team.

Age: 33
Weight at 21: 110 pounds
Weight today: 110 pounds

BREAKFAST

On most mornings Lili has a blender-mixed protein drink (the same drink as her husband, Richard). Then she has a dish of fresh fruit and a cup of regular tea. She does not have toast.

LUNCH

Lili always has a salad with either pasta, salmon, or tuna, and iced tea. She never drinks soft drinks. If tea or Perrier is not available (for example, at a baseball game), she would rather have a beer.

DINNER

Lili always eats dinner with Dick around 7:00 P.M. She has a green salad with steamed green vegetables, brown rice or potato, chicken or fish, and, twice a week, beef.

EXERCISE

Lili's workout schedule is forty-five minutes, five days a week, including fifteen or twenty minutes of aerobics and light weights.

COMMENTS

When Lili started producing movies, she found it extremely difficult to stay with her diet and exercise regimen while on location because of the difficult, long, and strenuous hours. Consequently, she got in the habit of weighing herself daily. While on location, Lili sometimes moves up three or four pounds, but she never allows it to go beyond that. Although Dick and Lili lead a very demanding social life and spend many nights out for dinner, they consistently eat dinner at 7:00 P.M. (before going out) and are very careful what they eat while they are out.

(continued)

Richard Zanuck

Dick, with his long-time partner David Brown, produced such blockbusters as *Jaws*, *The Sting*, *Butch Cassidy and the Sundance Kid*, and *Patton*.

Age: 52
Weight at 21:   135 pounds
Weight today: 135 pounds

BREAKFAST

Five days a week, Richard has a blender-mixed protein drink with ingredients such as supplemental barley green, potassium, ascorbate powder, and extract of sea vegetation. Occasionally he has some herbal tea at the office in the midmorning.

LUNCH

Richard always has a salad of some kind, preferably crab, shrimp, or seafood, with iced tea.

DINNER

Richard reports that his dinner is "a mixed bag, probably more beef than I should be having, but I try to mix it with chicken and fish as much as I can." Dick occasionally drinks a little champagne before dinner and usually has a glass of wine during dinner. He eats dinner as early as possible, but no later than 7:00 P.M.

Dick loves desserts, but holds them to special occasions.

EXERCISE

Richard completes a three-mile run seven days a week rain or shine (followed by a dip in the ocean) supplemented by half an hour, three days a week, of weight training. In addition, Dick plays tennis and skis.

COMMENTS

I'll let Dick speak for himself regarding his daily exercise: "I love my morning run," he says. "I can do a great deal of thinking in the solitude found at the beach at that hour. My mind is clearer than at any other time of the day, and I'm able to solve problems and think about things I would normally not have time for."

And, I might add, his running has kept him in great shape over the thirty-five years we've been friends.

◄ ◄ 16 ► ►

Shopping and Cooking Habits to Keep You in the Winner's Circle

Never has there been a greater choice of foods and as great a purchasing power to obtain those foods as there is in the United States today. Like any freedom, however, the ability to choose from a seemingly endless assortment of goodies has a responsibility: You have to exercise some self-restraint.

That can be tough, especially when the food industry spends billions annually in ads that try to convince us to do just the opposite. It's still possible to out-fox the Madison Avenue executives. All you need is to know a few tricks:

The Right Shopping Habits

1. *Never go grocery shopping when you're hungry.* This is important if you're going to resist the advertising and packaging temptations thrown at you at every turn of the grocery aisle. If you do end up at the grocery hungry, try this tip: Go find something healthy, and eat it while you shop. Peel a banana or munch on an apple. Then when you get to the checkout stand, tell them what you've eaten. They'll add a few cents to your bill, and that will be that. Most important, don't be intimidated—don't be concerned whether somebody is going to say something to you. (No one would give you a glance if you were eating an ice cream cone.)

Be Proud of Your New Eating Habits

When I shop for groceries, I nearly always eat a banana or other piece of fruit. If somebody sees me, I couldn't care less. I always pay for it, so what's the big deal.

In the same manner, don't be intimidated by a waiter or waitress when you ask for salad dressing on the side, or for your fish poached or broiled instead of fried. Don't be afraid to ask someone not to smoke.

Don't be intimidated by someone kidding you about eating brown rice or a plain baked potato.

When it comes to your weight and your health, be an uncommon man or woman. Don't worry about what the rest of the herd is doing. Be a leader—not a follower.

---

2. *Learn to read labels.* By FDA regulation, most foods must list their ingredients (the exceptions are "single-ingredient" foods such as flour or milk) in order of weight, with the major ingredient first.

   Learn to avoid certain ingredients, especially if they are near the top of the list (if they are a potent ingredient, such as salt, they don't even need to be near the head of the list to be avoided). Here are the ingredients you need to watch for:

   - Flour. Avoid bleached flour, and try to avoid enriched flour. Best is to find a bread made with simple whole-wheat flour. With a little diligence you can find breads with at least a high percentage of this good grain.
   - Saturated Fats. I talk more about fats on page 213. It's important to know what oils to avoid because certain ones cause harmful formation of cholesterol plaque in your arteries.

- Salt. This one can be tough because it can be positioned way down the ingredient list, and still be too much. If you're lucky, the product may list the milligrams (mg) of salt in the food. I would be cautious about any product showing over 100 milligrams of salt per serving. Keep in mind that studies have shown we can get by quite nicely on as little as 50 milligrams of salt per day.
- Preservatives. The jury is still out on the possibly carcinogenic effect of foods laden with preservatives. My view is better safe than sorry, especially when there's no reason to eat the kinds of foods that require big doses of preservatives to keep them from spoiling. Keep a wary eye out for any foods with a list of ingredients that looks more like the annual report for Dow Chemical than like something you should be putting in your body.
- Sugar. Reduce the amount of simple-sugar carbohydrates (as opposed to starch, or complex, carbohydrates) in your diet. Avoid foods with too high a percentage of simple sugars. Remember, simple sugar comes under a list of guises: dextrose, honey, corn syrup (and other kinds of syrup), molasses, brown sugar, malt, and maltose. Avoid artificial sweeteners, too. As with preservatives, there's controversy over whether or not these chemicals are carcinogenic, but there used to be a lot of controversy over whether or not cigarettes were carcinogenic. And now we know.

3. *Watch out for the words "organic" and "natural."*

As yet, there is no federal regulation over the use of these two words by the food industry and, believe me, many manufacturers take advantage of it. As any of you who took chemistry in school know, strictly speaking the word "organic" means any compound that contains carbon. In food, it means anything that any manufacturer wants to pawn off as good for you, whether it is or not. Same for the word "natural." In fact, I've developed a knee-jerk suspicion of any foods that use either of these two words in their promotion.

Fast-Food Miracles

Each spring food manufacturers in the United States convene at Chicago's McCormick Place to display their latest fast-food miracles. This huge trade show features up to 2,500 new items trying to compete for space on America's crowded grocery shelves.

Unfortunately, you'd have a hard time finding a real orange and apple in the place. The American food industry is more interested in products that fit under one buzzword: FAST. According to General Foods, the American consumer wants convenience like he or she has never had convenience before.

The Johnson company of Milwaukee rolled out a new hot fudge sundae that you nuke in the microwave and, schazaam, the ice cream stays cold and the fudge gets hot. General Foods says they have a new instant chicken à la king dinner that will keep in the fridge for a year. That'll save a few trips to the grocery store.

ABC Research, Inc., developed a prototype precooked steak with charcoal flavoring and fake grill marks. General Mills is doing research to see if the American public is psychologically ready to buy complete dinners off the dry shelf at the grocery.

Not all manufacturers are ignoring that part of the market interested in healthy eating. Just look at how many prepared foods co-opt the word "natural" or "organic."

Same with the word "homemade." At the last trade show one manufacturer had "homemade" written on precooked, packaged mesquite-smoked chicken that *Newsweek* magazine reported tasted like "a hot dog drenched in sugary butter-sauce".

If you want to be taken by the fast-food barkers, it's your funeral. As for me, I'll stick with wholesome foods prepared with simple recipes.

Not All Oils Are Created Equal

All oils are part of the class of foods called fats, and fats are an important source of food energy in our diets. But for most Americans, fat is too big a source of calories, and the high consumption of fat in the American diet is the leading cause of obesity.

Remember: Keep fats to less than 30 percent of your total calories.

It's also important that the majority of that 30 percent be from fats that are not harmful to you. These types of fats are in the form of oils, but there are good oils and bad oils. You need to learn the difference if you want to stay in the Winner's Circle.

Oils come in two general categories—saturated and unsaturated. The most visible difference between these two types is that at room temperature saturated oils are generally solid, and unsaturated oils are liquid.

As far as your health goes, you need to remember that saturated oils are the bad guys, and unsaturated oils are the good guys. Here's why: Chemically speaking, the difference between a saturated oil and an unsaturated one has to do with the number of hydrogen atoms bonded to the oil molecule. In terms of your body chemistry, the saturated fats, with more hydrogen, tend to increase your level of low-density lipoproteins (LDL), that agent responsible for the build-up of cholesterol on your arterial walls. Here's the bottom line:

Saturated fats increase your blood cholesterol level. Unsaturated fats, especially polyunsaturated fats, either have no effect or actually lower your blood cholesterol level.

What are saturated fats? Foremost, they are animal fats found in meat, dairy products, and lard. There are also two saturated fats from plant sources that you should know about: palm oil and coconut oil. *Coconut oil has a level of saturation 300 to 400 percent higher than pure beef fat.* In fact, it's the most saturated fat there is. It's also commonly used as an ingredient in packaged foods because it prevents spoiling (no wonder!). If there's one thing from this chapter you need to know, it's this: *Keep a weather eye open for coconut oil.* It's in hundreds of things you buy at the grocery store. You have to learn to avoid it.

How about unsaturated fats? Polyunsaturated fats have been shown to actually reduce serum cholesterol.

Here's a list of polyunsaturated oils in order of their nonsaturation, with the healthiest oils listed first.

Safflower Oil
Sunflower Oil
Corn Oil
Cottonseed Oil

Olive oil is a special case. It's called a monounsaturated oil, and studies have indicated that it not only helps lower overall serum cholesterol but also tends to lower LDL levels while leaving HDL levels unchanged. The studies are promising for this oil, which can be part of a healthy diet.

How to Shop for Good Oils

- Margarine. Choose margarines made completely from polyunsaturated fats. The best margarine is the kind made from safflower oil.
- Cooking and salad oils. Choose the ones made from polyunsaturated fats such as safflower, corn, or cottonseed oils (these oils are better than peanut oil, too). Avoid fats like Crisco, or any other cooking fat that is solid at room temperature.
- Breakfast cereals. Look out for cold cereals with too much fat or oil. Many of them have coconut oil, which is strictly taboo.
- Crackers and breads. Watch out for coconut oil, and look out for hydrogenated oils. Look for brands that use principally polyunsaturated oils.
- Cookies. You shouldn't be eating these anyway. If you do succumb, be aware that *most* of them are made with coconut oil *and* hydrogenated oil.

Be wary of the hydrogenated and partially hydrogenated oils. These Jekyll and Hyde culprits used to be good guys but have undergone a manufacturing conversion that has turned them into bad guys.

Hydrogenation is a process started in the food industry back in 1915 that adds hydrogen atoms to unsaturated fats, turning them into saturated ones. The food industry likes to do this because saturated fats are better preservatives, and they often give processed foods a firmer texture. Your body and health, though, are not in agreement with the food industry. You may notice that some oils are listed as "partially hydrogenated." These aren't as bad for you (hydrogenation is done in degrees), but in general these oils should be avoided. Be aware that most margarines and virtually all brands of commercially packaged breads, muffins, and baked goods contain hydrogenated oils.

A Few Tips on Cooking and Food Preparation

You can buy the most wholesome and nutritious foods and still blow it if you prepare them improperly. Good cooking habits are really important if you want to stay in the Winner's Circle. Here are a few tips:

1. Go easy on cooking oil. Use only the polyunsaturated varieties, and use them moderately. We've gotten used to a nonstick cooking spray called Pam, which is probably the most fat-free method of coating a skillet surface you can find.

2. Don't boil, steam. This guideline is very important when cooking vegetables. Steaming does not remove the vitamins and nutrients nearly to the degree that boiling does. If you don't have one, invest in a good steamer. I find the kind

with nesting baskets the most convenient—the interior baskets allow you to steam more than one item at a time.

3. Use a microwave to cook vegetables and fish. No water or oils need be used since the moisture in the food is enough.

4. There are good ways and bad ways to fry food. Generally speaking, try to substitute other cooking techniques for frying as much as possible. When you do fry, use only polyunsaturated oils, and use the absolute minimum amount.

5. Do not cook with heavy sauces or gravies. It's better simply to get out of the creamy-sauce habit. Stick to sauces made from polyunsaturated oils and vinegar. If you do prepare a sauce with milk or cheese, use low-fat or nonfat products.

6. Remove the skin from chicken *before* you cook it. This significantly reduces the amount of fat in the meat.

These tips on shopping and cooking habits will help you lose weight and maintain your ideal weight without a lot of calorie counting and extra thought.

There's one more thing I'd like to add. Buying unprocessed, naturally grown foods and vegetables is generally less expensive than paying for their adulterated, processed, packaged, and ballyhooed opposites. Eating healthy foods also reduces your doctor bills and waistline. It's a great investment no matter how you measure it.

John and Kathinka Tunney

John Tunney

John was formerly United States Senator from California and is now a successful real estate developer and TV political commentator.

Age: 52
Weight at 21: 185
Weight today: 179

BREAKFAST

John's basic breakfast includes an apple, two slices of dry toast, and oatmeal without milk. He drinks one cup of coffee.

LUNCH

John eats the same basic lunch every day: a tuna, chicken, or turkey sandwich on whole-wheat bread, with iced tea or mineral water.

DINNER

John eats from two basic dinner menus: pasta or fish with rice or potatoes, served with salad. He sometimes has a glass of wine with dinner. Occasionally he has ice cream for dessert, which is about the only dairy product he eats.

SNACKS

If he snacks, it's only on fruit. John says he listens to an inner clock that knows when he's gaining weight and tells him it's time to cut back on foods such as ice cream.

EXERCISE

John does twenty minutes of stretching and stomach exercises daily. He is a strong singles tennis player and also tries to keep up with Kathinka's skiing, a difficult assignment. John has a perpetually young look and outlook: He actually seems to be aging in reverse. This is a man who bounces when he walks and does everything with verve and élan.

Kathinka Tunney

Kathinka is a four-time Swedish National downhill-skiing champion and a 1962 World Cup competitor.

Age: 45
Weight at 21: 140
Weight today: 135

BREAKFAST

Kathinka alternates between two hot cereals (either Kashi or oatmeal)—both served with sliced apples. She doesn't drink coffee.

(continued)

LUNCH

Kathinka has four basic lunch menus: fruit salad, shrimp salad, tuna salad, or chicken salad. She usually drinks a glass of iced tea.

DINNER

Kathinka eats the same as John: salad and pasta or fish with brown rice or potatoes. She sometimes has a glass of wine.

EXERCISE

Kathinka tries to exercise four days a week, alternating between strenuous walking, swimming, biking, or aerobics.

COMMENTS

When she was competing in her early twenties, Kathinka weighed 140 pounds of solid muscle. In those days, the one thing she liked to do after training six hours a day was to indulge herself in those wonderful Viennese pastries.

Once she stopped racing, though, Kathinka instinctively knew she had to pay more attention to her eating habits. Several of her friends, however, continued eating the pastries long after they quit racing, and Kathinka is afraid that if they went skiing today and fell in the snow, they would make a very large indentation.

At age forty-five and three children later, Kathinka has been able to maintain her 135-pound, trim, and athletic figure by eating from a limited number of basic, nutritious menus and by following her exercise regimen. She is still active on the slopes and is one of the finest skiers, male or female, I've ever had the pleasure of trying to follow down the hill.

17

Special Occasions: Those Tough Times for New Habits

This chapter deals with those tough times when it's impossible to stick to your routine—times when your daily schedule is disrupted, when you fly in airplanes, when you eat at restaurants, when you face the challenge of getting through the holiday season without gaining weight. These are times that can try new habits if you aren't prepared. If you know how to handle special occasions, though, you can breeze right through without a single step outside the Winner's Circle.

Airline Meals: How to Survive Them

Airline meals are a joke. Recently the assistant director of cardiology at Washington Hospital Center was so appalled at the breakfast and lunch he was served on a flight that he put it in a bag and took it to his lab for analysis. The result: The two-meal breakdown was 2,600 calories, with 66 percent from fat, and had a total of 900 milligrams of cholesterol. The American Heart Association (and *The 7-Week Victory Diet*) recommend that your meals have no more than 30 percent fat and that your daily intake of cholesterol not exceed 300 milligrams.

Let's face it, air travel is a hazard to your new eating habits and a hazard to your health, but you don't have to be trapped in the air with only airline meals. You *can* do something about it. You can take your own food.

The rule for healthy air travel is: *Pack a picnic*. Make your flight a festive occasion. If you really want to feel deluxe, get a wicker basket small enough to fit under an airline seat. Pack it with a checked-cloth place mat to use as a tablecloth (they're the size of the fold-down trays on the backs of airplane seats), napkins, plates, forks and spoons (no knives—you can't get them through security). Then for breakfast, pack small boxes of Shredded Wheat or Kellogg's All-Bran. For lunch pack a tuna or turkey sandwich (either also makes a healthy dinner). Take a delicious selection of fruit for dessert and snacks.

There's one other rule for air travel you absolutely must follow: *Take your own water*. I can't emphasize how important this is. The interior air in a plane is extremely dry, and it is also pressurized to an altitude of about 5,000 feet. Both factors dehydrate you. The thinner air makes you breathe more frequently, and because the air is dry, you lose moisture through your lungs.

For these reasons you should *guzzle* water when you're flying. You will have a hard time getting any flight attendant to bring you the amount of water you need. That's why I always take with me a couple of plastic bottles of water (such as Evian). Drinking plenty of water will keep you from getting constipated—a common flying problem caused by dehydration —and helps to reduce the effects of jet lag.

Restaurants: How to Eat Out

I've often heard people complain that they would like to lose weight by eating healthy food but that because of their business or social obligations they frequently eat in restaurants and they think it's just impossible. On the other hand, part of the fun of seeing friends is exploring new restaurants and new tastes. There is a way to eat properly and remain true to a winning lifestyle. There's no reason on earth why you can't go to restaurants and still follow all the eating habits outlined in *Win the Food Fight*. In fact, there are only four rules you have to follow.

1. Never eat in a junk restaurant or a restaurant where you can't get at least a good salad.
2. Choose meals that are as close as you can get to your basic Victory Menus.
3. If nothing on the menu comes close, go to the salad bar. (But watch what you put on your salad!)
4. In a fancy restaurant order just hors d'oeuvres. My wife and I have done this for years. Meals are light, tasty, and very satisfying.

A close friend recently opened a very upscale restaurant and invited us to the opening party. It was on the house, so most people went for the chops, steak, and veal. On close inspection, however, the menu offered some terrific hors d'oeuvres. We ordered a very thin but large slice of delicious raw sea bass marinated lightly with herbs. We followed that with fresh, mixed, chopped salad (dressing on the side) and finished with a light potato pancake topped with a dab of crème-fraîche and a slice of Scotch salmon. We indulged on the cream but there wasn't that much of it. We finished this appetizing meal with a delicious glazed pear for dessert. It was a great dinner meal without too many excess calories.

There are many variations on the hors d'oeuvres dinner. Try it sometime, for a trim way to have fun and feel very satisfied.

That's all there is to it. Commit those four rules to memory, and I guarantee you'll be able to eat out and not gain weight. Let me give you an example of how it's done.

Recently I went out to dinner with a business associate, and just out of interest I kept track of everything he ate versus everything I ate. Basically, we both had salads, he had a steak and potato for an entrée and I had pasta. We both had dinner rolls, and we both had dessert. I was curious to know what the real difference was between the two meals, so when I got home I got out my copy of *The Nutritive Value of American Foods* (published by the Department of Agriculture and available from the Government Printing Office, Washington, D.C.) and broke down the two dinners into their nutritional components. This isn't something I usually do because I never keep track of calories. The results, which are shown on the following pages, were revealing.

	Calories	Fat (in grams)	Carbo-hydrates (in grams)	Protein (in grams)
Handful of nuts	100	9.5	3.0	3.0
Half avocado with	188	18.5	7.1	2.4
shrimp and	120	6.1	2.8	11.0
mayonnaise	200	22.0	0.6	0.4
Club steak	750	65.0	—	34.0
Baked potato	145	0.2	33.0	4.0
Sour cream	125	11.2	1.2	2.0
Three pats butter	108	12.5	—	—
One dinner roll	105	1.6	19.1	3.2
Serving of peas	109	18.9	0.5	3.2
Cream for coffee	40	3.5	1.4	1.0
Chocolate mint	100	3.0	20.0	0.5
Totals	2,090	172.0	88.7	64.7

Of those 2,090 calories, 12 percent came from protein, 17 percent from carbohydrate, and 71 percent from fat (fat has twice has many calories per gram as either protein or carbohydrate).

MY DINNER

	Calories	Fat (in grams)	Carbo-hydrate (in grams)	Protein (in grams
Lettuce	10	0.1	2.2	0.7
Oil & vinegar dressing	66	6.2	2.8	0.1
One-half tomato	13	0.1	2.8	0.7
Pasta with	192	0.7	39.1	6.5
tomato sauce and	88	0.4	20.0	3.8
Parmesan cheese	111	7.4	0.8	10.2
Whole-wheat roll	84	1.9	14.2	2.2
with margarine	27	3.1	—	—
One glass white wine	87	—	4.3	0.1
One cup decaf coffee	2	—	—	—
with lowfat milk	10	0.5	1.8	1.3
Brownie with nuts	97	6.3	10.2	1.3
Totals	787	26.7	98.2	26.9

Of those 787 calories, 16 percent came from protein, 52 percent from carbohydrate, and 32 percent from fat. Quite a difference from my friend's dinner, isn't it? Simply sticking close to one of the basic recipes I eat all the time on the Victory Diet allowed me to choose a restaurant meal with about one-third the calories of my friend's. My meal was just as filling as his, and to my way of thinking, better tasting. I even splurged on an indulgent dessert.

What if there isn't anything on the menu close to one of your basic recipes? In that case, head for the salad bar, but be careful! Salad bars are full of fats and oils that you have to learn to avoid.

How to Eat at a Salad Bar

Salad bars can be the restaurant-goer's best friend. You've got to learn to avoid all the fats and oils, though. Here are a few tips.

1. Never use the heavy cream dressings. Always choose the oil-and-vinegar kinds of dressings, and use them in *small* amounts.

2. Never eat macaroni salads heavy with creamy dressings. These often contain mayonnaise and have terribly high amounts of fat. You're better off choosing a pasta salad made with olive oil or vegetable oil. If you're not sure what's in a certain dressing, don't be afraid to ask!

3. Never mix the ingredients into a big garbage pile of food. Place your salad-bar choices in discrete areas of your plate, and make choices that complement one another. You'll find that if you take care with your selections and arrange them on the plate, you'll enjoy your salad more, and you will probably eat it more slowly, which is much better for your digestion. Here are a few good foods to look for at a salad bar:

Fresh raw broccoli and cauliflower
Cherry tomatoes
Celery and carrot sticks
Fresh spinach and lettuce
Fresh cabbage
Whole-grain breads (plain or spread with only margarine)
Cucumbers
Radishes
Garbanzo beans
Raisins
Sunflower seeds
Red and green bell peppers

Junk Restaurants Serve Junk Food

One of the three rules for eating out is to try to avoid junk restaurants. Avoid those fried-food joints where the only vegetables in the house are the people standing in line waiting for their leather hamburgers. Believe me, you won't find anything close to the basic recipes you're used to, and the chances are you won't find a salad bar, either.

The Wisdom of Eating by Candlelight

When I was at Stanford, I worked as a hasher (busboy) at Robley Hall, residence of about 700 freshman co-eds. The noise level was high, the dishes rattled, and we didn't help matters any with our busing.

Every Wednesday night, though, the co-eds were required to dress for dinner, and there was candlelight in the dining hall. The change between Tuesday evening and Wednesday evening was staggering. The candlelight brought the noise level down to where you could almost whisper. Everybody seemed to be in a much better mood on Wednesday evening. There was no rushing and hassling, only pleasant conversation. I always regretted that every night couldn't be Wednesday, and now, whenever possible, I always choose to eat in restaurants that have quiet, peaceful surroundings.

That doesn't mean you have to eat in expensive restaurants. If you look around, you can find plenty of reasonable places that have either a few selections on their menus close to the Victory Menus, or a good salad bar.

I'm convinced one reason people in this country eat so poorly is because they never really satisfy their taste buds with good food. If you eat a good meal in a good restaurant, it should give you pleasure that lingers for hours. Have you ever stuffed yourself at a junk restaurant, then later had pleasant thoughts and memories about your meal? Highly unlikely.

Avoid junk restaurants, eat by candlelight, stick close to your basic Victory Recipes, and learn to head for the salad bar in a pinch. I guarantee that if you oblige these tenets, you'll lose weight and you'll be quite satisfied.

There's just one problem. If you're like me, you'll still have a kind of crazed desire every once in a while for something totally off the charts from your regular eating habits.

How to Pig Out

Once you've reached your target weight, once you are happily and healthfully addicted to your new eating habits, your desire for your old foods will diminish. Still, you may now and then feel the urge to indulge in some of your previous eating habits. That's okay: Once in a while, you need to go off the deep end.

Nobody should be too authoritarian; nobody should be a Food Nazi. Life's too short for anything less. Here are two of my favorite pig-outs.

1. *French Toast.* I love this stuff, and I have it two or three Sunday mornings a month. Sunday is my pig-out day. Since I've been eating well the rest of the week, it doesn't hurt me, either. Besides, Sunday is usually the day when I get more exercise, so I burn off a lot of the extra sugar.

If I really wanted to be careful (if I were overweight and trying to get used to my new eating habits), I would still splurge on French toast on Sunday mornings, but I would make it using Ann Hand's favorite low-calorie recipe. (Ann is profiled on page 174.) Make the batter using a single egg (or two egg whites and one yolk), skim milk, and a dash each of cinnamon and nutmeg. Soak the bread in the batter, then cook it in a pan coated with Pam nonstick cooking spray. I would go ahead and use maple syrup in very moderate amounts (maple syrup is more expensive, but because its taste is stronger, it's easier to use sparingly).

2. *The Big Bubba Burger*. Maybe once every couple of months I'll go all out on a Big Bubba Burger (or its immoral equivalent, available at any burger stand). Big Bubbas (a burger with the works—pickles, mayo, ketchup, cheese, tomato, onion, etc.) are out of the stadium as far as the Winner's Circle goes, but a splurge now and then is good for the soul. You should know, however, that there's enough grease in a Big Bubba to fill all the lube racks at Indianapolis.

Once I chomp into a Big Bubba, though, I can't really say it tastes as good as I thought it would (my body has been away from these things too long to be able to take the heavy fat shock without protesting). It does, however, take care of my craving to pig out. After a Big Bubba, I go right back to the Victory Diet guidelines, quite happy to stay there for another couple of months.

Holiday Eating

It's okay to pig out once in a while, but the holiday seasons are a special challenge because if you cut loose from Christmas week right through New Year's Eve, you'll be hurting. Holiday eating also includes birthdays, weddings, anniversaries, company parties, bar mitzvahs, Independence Day, Labor Day, Memorial Day, Washington's Birthday, Lincoln's Birthday, and Quredwin Galumpchick's Birthday.

How I Get Through Shirley Turtletaub's New Year's Day Extravaganza

Although I certainly have been to my share of celebrations, the one that sticks out in my mind is a New Year's Day extravaganza that my wife and I have been going to for ten years running. It's a feast put on by an old friend, Shirley Turtletaub, the quintessential "eat now, talk later" Jewish mother who lovingly plans this event for weeks in advance.

Just a sample—not all, mind you, but just a sample—of what she had on her table last New Year's Day included four pounds of Nova Scotia salmon (lox), a bucket full of Greek black olives, a slug of kosher dill pickles, some sensational creamy coleslaw, a giant bowl of knockout salad, a plate of delicious cold chicken, slices of hot brisket in gravy, whitefish, gefilte fish, smoked fish, broiled fish, big kosher franks, mounds of mayonnaise, four kinds of mustard, exotic condiments. . . .

I could go on and on. When you see how terrific the table looks, you feel like you could just eat for five hours while watching back-to-back bowl games.

But there is a way to cover your temptation. Of all those dishes I mentioned, which do you think I go for? The cold chicken, the green salad, and a smidgen of Nova Scotia salmon on rye. By the time I'm through eating these, the brisket, the hot dog, and the cole-slaw all of a sudden don't look so hot.

Besides, I've got to save room for dessert.

If you want to go crazy, let me tell you about the dessert table. Two huge homemade chocolate cakes, a gorgeous pumpkin pie with homemade whipped cream, a splendiferous carrot cake, a bucket of sensational homemade chocolate chip cookies, and eight pints of Häa-gen-Dazs. Next to that, the coffee urn.

The visual aspect of this galaxy of desserts is so dazzling that most people just dive in. If you play your cards right, though, you can be just as happy and just as satisfied by nibbling on a little piece of cake and taking a little sip of coffee.

With that, you've just made it through Shirley's New Year's extravaganza, no worse for wear. Of course, on the way out she will always say, "But you didn't eat a thing!!"

Here are a few tips to get you through the entire holiday season without breaking the bathroom scales come January 2:

1. Eat turkey. In fact, you should eat turkey for more than just the holidays. It's a wonderful source of protein with virtually no fat.

2. Eat turkey *without gravy*. Gravy is so high in fat that you can eat an entire day's worth of calories in just a few ladles full. Instead of gravy, spread a little low-sugar cranberry sauce on the meat. It's a wonderful combination.

3. Avoid traditional stuffing. Turkey stuffing is made with butter, oil, fat, and salt. You can make a good low-fat stuffing, though. Jane Brody's *Good Food Book* has a terrific recipe for low-fat apple-raisin stuffing that I'll bet you'll enjoy more than the old-style stuffing you're used to.

4. Avoid eggnog, made with or without alcohol. Have fruit juice and mineral water, instead, or, if you must have alcohol, try rum and fruit juice.

5. Avoid anything made with quantities of butter.

6. Eat plenty of vegetables, and eat potatoes and sweet potatoes only with safflower oil margarine.

If you follow these simple guidelines, you won't *feel* deprived at Christmas, Thanksgiving, or New Year's because you won't *be* deprived. Your holiday meal will be every bit the feast of a traditional one, and you'll stay within the Winner's Circle of acceptable foods.

Mariel Hemingway

Mariel, new mother and actress, and her husband, Steve Crissman, are well-known restaurateurs in New York City.

Age: 25

Mariel gave us the following information 4½ months into her pregnancy.

BREAKFAST

Five to six days a week Mariel has oatmeal, with a piece of whole-grain toast and no butter. On weekends she often makes her own bran-batter waffles and eats them with a very small amount of syrup and no butter or margarine. During pregnancy she did not drink any tea or coffee—only water.

LUNCH

On most days Mariel makes a vegetable sandwich: whole-wheat bread, avocado, sprouts, onion, tomato, and lettuce (no mayonnaise).

DINNER

Nearly every day Mariel eats a huge green salad, and then fish or chicken. She completely refrained from alcohol during her pregnancy.

(continued)

EXERCISE

Each day Mariel swims or takes a brisk walk for at least an hour.

COMMENTS

Mariel is very careful about what she eats. She had no odd cravings during pregnancy, except one yearning for a toasted cheese sandwich, which she had never eaten before. So she ate one, and that was that. During her pregnancy she continued to avoid dairy products other than the skim milk she has on her oatmeal. She got the extra calcium she needed during pregnancy from eating salmon (high in calcium), and by taking a calcium supplement.

Mariel's baby, Dree, is a happy, always smiling, beautiful young lady who is already piggybacking on her mother's long walks.

How to Get Your
Kids to Follow Your
New Habits

It's tougher now for a kid to eat well and exercise correctly than it was when I was a kid. I didn't have to fight the siren call of McDonald's and What-A-Burger; I didn't have a kaleidoscope of sugar-frosted breakfast cereals taking up full aisles of the grocery when I went shopping with my mother; there weren't fast-food manufacturers with $100-million ad budgets to lure me into bad eating habits; and at school the physical education programs hadn't been cut by budget reductions to the point of being hollow shams.

That's not to say my eating habits as a kid were completely healthy. My parents fed me for breakfast sugared cereal, bacon and eggs, white bread, and butter. My school served the wrong lunch, and when I got home my mom told me not to eat early because I'd spoil my dinner.

She had no idea that I *should* be spoiling my dinner.

She had no idea that there's nothing more harmful for kids' health than that old refrain: Get your hand out of the icebox— you'll spoil your dinner! Even if a kid is reaching for fruit! You'll spoil your dinner!

Why? Because kids and everybody else should eat when they're hungry. "You'll spoil your dinner" is out of date and tragically wrong.

Most days, my kids eat their dinner between 3:30 and 4:30 in the afternoon, when they're the hungriest. They've been at school all day running, jumping, pushing, kicking, shouting, and (we hope) studying, so when they get home they're starved, and that's when they eat. So what if they spoil their dinner? They still sit at the table when the rest of us eat (no later than 6:00). They nibble a little at the table, and maybe a little more before bedtime, but when breakfast comes around *they are ready*—ready for a big meal that gives them the foundation they need to make it through the day and that prevents them from overeating at lunch.

Eating too much of the wrong food at lunch was the other big problem I had as a kid. Earlier in the book I told you how I always nodded off in my 1:00 class because I had a case of the afternoon doldrums. If I'd known more about nutrition, I would have rocketed through the entire school day full of energy.

Don't Pass Your Bad Eating Habits to Your Children

If you are overweight, chances are you're that way not because you inherited bad genes but because you inherited bad eating habits. If you are overweight and you have a fond regard for your mother's cooking, chances are that her cooking is close to the Standard American Diet. Why? The chances are that your mother had far less nutritional knowledge available to her than you do.

That's not the worst of it. If you picked up bad eating habits from your parents, your health is probably in more jeopardy today than theirs was at a similar age. Why? Because they didn't have a galaxy of frosted breakfast cereals and fast-food restaurants to choose from. They didn't have to wander down grocery aisles overflowing with chips, spreads, snacks, cookies, and other highly sugared, highly salted, partially hydrogenated junk food.

With more and more instant food products available each year, it's increasingly important that we learn healthy eating habits so we can walk through the grocery store minefield without destroying our health. It's more and more important that we do something not only to adopt good eating habits for ourselves but also to pass those habits on to our children so that we can break the generation-to-generation chain of bad eating habits that is keeping our country imprisoned in a fortress of fat.

The Health of Our Children: Bad and Getting Worse

Before we discuss how to improve our children's health, let's take a brief look at just how bad their health is.

A recent issue of the *American Journal of Diseases of Children* reported that the proportion of kids in America who are overweight has increased 50 percent in the last twenty years. Fifty percent! The Harvard School of Public Health found that the number is even higher among children aged six to eleven. A Lou Harris poll reveals that 40 percent of kids aged five to eight have elevated blood pressure. A recent article in *Time* magazine reported on the slackening physical fitness of

America's kids: "Forty percent of boys and 70 percent of girls cannot do more than a single pull-up." Only seventeen states in the country have mandatory physical education programs. Only one-third of all students nationwide take such classes. But get this one: *Kids spend an average of twenty-four hours a week in front of the television, and during much of that time they are snacking on junk food.*

Although the health of the adults in America seems to be improving, that of the children is worsening. It's clear to me that as a nation we aren't passing our eating and exercise habits on to our kids. The following sections suggest ways you can take control and do something about this national crisis.

Set a Good Example

The single most important thing you can do to get your children to adopt good eating habits is to adopt those habits yourself. You know how much your kids copy your actions, gestures, and speech. They will also copy your eating habits if you present those habits as something positive and worth emulating.

There's no secret to getting your children to follow good eating habits when you follow those habits yourself. Our son Johnny doesn't eat steak, for example, because we never serve it. When we go to a restaurant, he never orders it because he doesn't think it's *the* thing on the menu. He's that way *not* because we beat it into his head, but because he grew up around people who reinforced the wisdom of good eating habits.

That's not to say, though, that he doesn't have a hamburger or pizza once in a while after his soccer games. We would be fools to deny him that because there would be no better prescription for rebellion. The last thing you want to be is a diet dictator. You've got to allow your kids to pig out on junk food once in a while.

It also helps to know that not all junk food places have the same bottom line. If you had a choice between going to McDonald's or Pizza Hut, for example, which one would you choose? Is there really a difference?

At McDonald's suppose we go for the McDLT burger with fries and a milkshake. Here's what we end up with:

Total calories: 1,300
Total percentage of calories that are fat: 46 percent
Total salt: 1,400 milligrams

With one hamburger you get between a third to a half of all the calories you probably need to eat in a day. With one hamburger, you are 16 percent over your limit for the percentage of calories you should be getting from fat. And one hamburger provides twenty-eight times your minimum daily requirement for salt, assuming you didn't salt your fries!

Now let's go to Pizza Hut, order their thin-and-crispy cheese pizza, and eat two slices. What do we end up with?

Total calories: 340
Total percentage of calories that are fat: 29 percent
Total salt: 924 milligrams

Obviously, we're much better off at Pizza Hut, even though we are still in the megadose range on salt. (Unfortunately, it is nearly impossible to avoid salt when you indulge in an occasional fast-food pig-out, but at least you should know about it so you can keep your kids on a healthier meal plan as much of the time as you can. There is no doubt kids eat too much salt: One recent study showed that the average American 4-year-old eats almost as much salt as an average teenager.)

The secret, then, is to allow your kids junk food once in a while, so they don't rebel and go on a junk-food binge as soon as they can pedal their bikes to the nearest hamburger stand.

Try to steer them toward the healthier fast-food places, and try to persuade them to follow good eating habits—your eating habits—by setting a positive example.

Here are nine additional tips to use in coaxing your kids to follow good eating habits:

1. Make mealtime light, cheery, and fun. Eliminate distractions so you can focus on your meal. Turn off the TV and turn on the soft sounds and good old-fashioned dialogue. Pleasant music and good conversations help you eat more slowly.

2. Explain to your kids why the food they are eating is good for them, even if they are young. Five-year-olds are savvy enough to get a sense of what vitamins, minerals, and complex carbohydrates are about, and if you keep telling them broccoli will make them strong, they'll believe you. But remember, you can't get your kids to follow good eating habits by intimidation: "Eat that broccoli or I'm going to break your neck" won't get you anywhere. Be patient and positive.

3. Let them help you prepare meals. If they've helped chop the broccoli (even a youngster can chop broccoli tops with a serrated plastic picnic knife), they'll be much more excited about eating it.

4. Never force a child to eat anything he doesn't like. Never ask him or her to clean the plate (and don't give the line about starving kids in China). *It's okay to leave some food uneaten.*

5. Coax your kids to give up soft drinks or, better still, don't let them get started. Instead, offer them different fruit juices cut with mineral water. My favorites are cranberry, apple, and white grape juice, all in 50/50 portions with mineral water.

6. Make sure the milk they drink is low-fat or nonfat, and use safflower oil margarine. They won't care about the differ-

ence after the first week. Kids react to fats just the way you do, and the less fat they eat, the less taste they'll have for high-fat foods. The same is true for sugar—the less they eat, the less they'll want.

7. Wean your children off the TV habit. TV has a peculiar ability to bore and mesmerize us at the same time, and it's a lethal combination because it also has the ability to lure us into snacking on junk food. Set TV time during the day and *stick to it. Don't ever let kids eat while watching.*

8. Remember, you have almost total control over what your kids eat up to age five, so get them started early with the right eating habits.

9. Make sure your kids eat dinner early. Children need to eat even earlier than adults because their stomachs are smaller and their metabolisms higher (kids have a much higher surface-to-volume ratio than adults). That means kids need to eat more frequently. By the time they get home from school, they are usually ready for dinner, and you shouldn't deny them. For the same reason, make sure you always have healthy snack foods around the house. More than anyone, children need to snack between meals. So keep that fruit bowl full on the table.

Another reason kids need to eat earlier than adults is that they go to bed earlier. Going to bed on a full stomach can lead to poor digestion and a tendency to gain weight. By allowing your kids to eat dinner after coming home from school, you give them a chance to digest their meal by bedtime at 8:00 to 9:00.

Tell 'Em to Brush Their Teeth, but Also Tell 'Em to Stand Up Straight and Drink Plenty of Water

What's the last thing most kids in America hear from their parents before they go to sleep? Is it "I love you" or "Did you say your prayers" or "Sleep tight"? No, it's "Did you brush your teeth?"

The toothpaste lobby couldn't have planned it better. I don't want to minimize the importance of brushing teeth before bedtime, but I do want to emphasize the importance of adding two other guiding principles to the list. It's equally important to tell your kids the following throughout every day:

1. Stand up straight.
2. Drink plenty of water.

Back pain and bone and joint problems are often caused by incorrect posture, and bad posture often starts with bad childhood habits.

Most kids start off with straight backs. Then they get a little older and their shoulders slump. By the time they're in their thirties, they start to get a pot gut that throws their backbone out of line even more. By the time they're in their forties, they're slump-shouldered and stooped.

I can't emphasize enough how important it is to get your kids to stand up straight. It will save them a lifetime of pain and disease.

Even more, standing up straight will help them be more successful, whatever they do. Why? Because bad posture leads to a hangdog, defeated appearance. And believe me, if you are applying for a job, making a presentation, or trying to sell somebody something, you're going to have a lot better chance if you're standing tall and looking proud.

Now wouldn't you want your kids to have that edge when they go out into the world?

The other important habit you've got to indoctrinate in your kids is to drink water. There's no single better habit advocated by the Victory Diet than drinking five to six glasses of water a day. And the easiest way to develop a water-drinking habit that will last a lifetime is to drink water as a kid.

This habit will not only lead to good adult habits, but also will ensure your child's health during his growing years, and will reduce any craving for soda.

And Now a Word from Our College Senior

On the chance that some of you may have college-age students, I give you permission to rip out the following pages written by our college-age son and pass them along.

I should mention, before you read this insert by Jim, that he is 6 feet 1 inch, 165 pounds with a body-fat content of 5 percent. I don't expect him to sustain that thirty years from today, but he's off to a great start.

Jim is a world-class white-water kayaker, a former National Junior-Olympic slalom champion, and holds a 3.5 grade average. (If a proud father can't brag, who can?)

Successful Eating at College
by Jim Grossman

As every student knows, eating at school can be difficult. Everywhere you turn you see unattractive and unappetizing meals; it's a far cry from mom's homecooked meals. The school cafeteria is your worst culinary nightmare fulfilled.

College food is generally overcooked, underflavored, and unnutritious—just like the food they served in high school, only now you are supposed to eat it three times a day. This institutional pablum only hastens students to the lure of the local pizza shop for pepperoni and sausage with extra grease, or to the nearest fast-food joint for a burger and Coke. Free from parental guidelines, many college students embark on a fast-food heyday.

But there is hope. There is a way to eat a healthy diet, to get three or four square meals a day. If a student is food smart and looks carefully, the school cafeteria does harbor a few things that at least won't poison him.

You've got to be discriminating. At breakfast they serve grease disguised as bacon and eggs, but they may also serve a steamer of oatmeal. Stick with this or cold cereal, but avoid the sugary brands. Bread is good, too, so long as it has color to it. If you've got a case of the morning-after dehydration syndrome, a big glass of O.J. is prescribed. Or try the fresh grapefruit or bananas that go mostly unnoticed by other students.

As for getting going the morning after an all-night study or party session, coffee is still the favorite. Most people's coffee addictions start in college, and it would be nice to stop the problem at the root. Unfortunately, most students do not have the foresight to nip the habit in the bud. Therefore, a few hints for morning drinking: Have the first (and I hope only) cup *with* breakfast. Try to avoid more coffee at midmorning, even if you have to weather "Application of Spectrology to Studies of Atmospheric Science" followed by "Constitution and the Culture of Constitutionalism."

On to lunch and dinner. At the school cafeterias, these two meals are usually identical. You are offered a selection of two or three equally unappetizing main dishes; skip any entrée that is indistinguishable in content or origin. If you can't tell what it is, you probably don't want to eat it. Look for meals high in complex carbohydrates—pasta, rice, beans. The vegetables they serve may have once been good for you, but in all likelihood they now have had the flavor, texture, and nutrition canned, processed, or cooked out of them. Go ahead and eat them if you like (I don't *think* they do more harm than good). And remember: There's always the salad bowl if the cooked veggies look too worn out.

Students often eat four meals a day. That last one occurs after you've had a 6:00 dinner, procrastinated a couple of hours, started studying for your Psych final at 8:00, then hit a blood-sugar low about midnight. You need a food fix fast to reverse that law of diminishing returns you learned about in Econ 101.

Your only hope here is to plan ahead. Figure that the little refrigerator in your dorm is for something other than stockpiling beer, and load it with fruit, nonfat milk, and some whole-grain cereal such as Shredded Wheat or Nutri-Grain. A bowl of this will get you through most cramming sessions.

That, then, is my plan for twenty-four hours of on-campus eating. What if you want to go off campus? What if nothing turns you on at the cafeteria? Don't panic. Try to find a good spot for *nongreasy* pizza (the kind made with little or no meat and plenty of veggies) or head for a fast-food restaurant with a good salad bar.

Wendy's is a nutritional oasis in the vast desert of fast-food restaurants. They have been uniquely innovative in offering healthy and nutritious food in a junk-food-dominated industry.

The especially health-conscientious person can choose a plain baked potato and the all-you-can-eat salad bar. The salad bar ranks with those found in top restaurants. The lettuce is consistently fresh, and the other items varied and numerous. Stay away from the oily prepared pasta salad and the pudding they put out to attract less religious palates.

Go heavy on tomatoes, bell peppers, sprouts, red onions, mushrooms, cucumbers, celery, carrots, and other fresh veggies. Top off with some vinegar, a squeeze of lemon, and some grated Parmesan cheese. Your plain baked potato can be made into a meal by adding your favorite vegetables.

For those looking to let loose and have a binge, Wendy's

does its best to make it healthy. Start out with a bowl of their favorite chili (it sets you free) instead of fries or chicken nuggets. If you are still craving a big, greasy burger, at least Wendy's offers it on a whole-wheat bun. But be prepared for nasty looks from the health-conscious clientele, especially the good-looking ones from the women's cross-country and volleyball teams!

Get Your Kid Out Running (or Skiing, Bicycling, Hiking . . .)

A recent Harris poll showed that a third of all boys and half of all girls six to seventeen years old can't run a mile in less than ten minutes. That's bad, really bad. Kids that age should be able to burn up the track. Instead, they're spending their time in front of the TV. George Allen, former head coach of the Los Angeles Rams and now chairman of the President's Council on Physical Fitness and Sports, says he has a study that shows kids watch TV or listen to the radio an average of twenty-four hours a week. Allen says TV addiction is one of the big reasons for lack of physical conditioning of America's youth, but he also blames the lack of physical education programs in schools.

We *have* to educate kids about the values of proper health and nutrition. We *have* to spend as much time on that part of a child's education as we do on the academic side. To favor academics and ignore health and fitness is a terrible, terrible, mistake. You might give a kid the best education in the world, and at thirty-five he or she might be the brightest person in the world, but it won't mean anything if he or she has a sore back, kidney problems, is stressed out and has high blood pressure, and is well on the way to a heart attack. What a total waste of a good education!

As a parent, you may not be able to find adequate exercise programs at your child's school. What can you do? Setting a good example is foremost. We have to instill in our kids the idea that exercise is valuable. We have to convince them that to look good and to feel good they have to follow good eating and exercise habits.

This, of course, isn't always easy to do. Sometimes you have to be subtle. Like many parents, I sometimes think kids are genetically encoded to rebel and do the opposite of whatever it is we want them to do. I also think that if we show our kids open love, and in that way win their trust and confidence, we can gently persuade them to follow our lead toward a lifetime of good eating and exercise habits.

If you have children, from newborns to teenagers, what is the greatest gift you can give them? Is it the estate, the trust, the business, the "best" education? No. The greatest thing, the thing no amount of money can buy, is health. If you want to leave your children with a single legacy that will more than anything else help them lead a happy and successful life, give them good eating and good exercise habits! A little later on in their lives they will thank you, over and over.

The Big Picture

The *7-Week Victory Diet* will work for you whether you're five years old or seventy-five. If you're seventy-five and you've never been concerned about nutrition, follow this book. It's never too late. If you're thirty-five and have a 7-year-old child and have never been interested in nutrition, follow this book because you've got twice the reason to do it: for yourself and for your child.

The earlier you start good eating and exercise habits, the better. It's never too late to change your life.

On my next birthday I'll be sixty. People say I look fit, trim, and healthy, and honestly I don't feel a day over thirty-five. Thirty-five is the way I think, the way I feel, and, consequently, the way I am. As that "great philosopher" Satchel Page said, "How old would you be if you didn't know how old you was?"

Please don't get me wrong. I don't want to sound like I'm waving a flag telling you how great I look and feel. What I *am* trying to do is give you a sense of the joy I have in life because of my good health so that you'll have the desire to change a few habits that will bring the same joy into your life.

Good health is the most valuable asset you can have. Money doesn't mean much if you can't stick around to enjoy it.

Remember the case of Edgar Bronfman, one of the richest men in the world, who has discovered health is worth more than anything else. If there's one lesson to learn from the Winner's Circle profiles in this book, it's this: Smart eating knows no social or economic boundaries. Anyone can win the food fight. All it takes is substituting a few new Victory Habits for your old bad habits. The process is easy, and with the help of this book, you can be in the Winner's Circle in just seven weeks.

The emphasis on good health in America seems to be increasing. The 1988 Surgeon General's *Report on Nutrition and Health* has been hailed as a landmark event equal to the 1964 report linking cigarette smoking to lung cancer. The rate of coronary disease, although still staggeringly high, has finally started to reverse direction. More people are exercising. The beef industry is in trouble. Our supermarkets have increasingly better selections of healthier food.

We are inching toward a healthier, more fat-free society, and I believe the momentum is gaining. In my mind, that makes it even more obvious that you don't want to get left behind. You've got to trade your bad habits for good eating habits *today*.

Now you've read the book—now you know that changing those habits is really quite easy. It's like acquiring a taste for a new food. The new habits—the new "taste"—may seem strange until you get used to it, but after a while you'll be hooked and you'll never want to go back to your old ways. Remember, when you've successfully changed your habits, when they have become time-tested old habits that work for you instead of against you, you won't want to deviate. You might not have Jim Palmer's head of hair or Clint Eastwood's knock-'em-dead stare, but you will have their vitality and good health.

You will also have a new way of thinking about yourself. You will feel better about life because you will look better. You will have put yourself in charge of your body instead of the other way around. This simple fact will inspire confidence that will carry over to everything else you do.

You will be in the Winner's Circle, steering the course and shape not only of your body but also of your entire life.

NO MORE EXCUSES. GO FOR IT. WIN THE FOOD FIGHT.

Acknowledgments

I've always wondered about acknowledgment pages and why authors include them in the first place. After spending almost three years on this book I can clearly see why most authors include thank yous. It's the least you can do for the enormous number of talented people who have spent a tremendous amount of time making the book possible. So at the risk of sounding like an Academy Award acceptance speech, here's my list of people whose help, assistance, advice, and guidance have been immeasurable. I hope I haven't forgotten anyone: Barbara Anderson and Nancy Coffey, great senior editors of St. Martin's Press; public relations genius Michael Schwager and his staff; Harvey Mackay, author of *Swim with the Sharks Without Being Eaten Alive,* who was kind enough to share his experiences in launching a book; title experts Wes Janz and Vicki Abrahamson; David Brown, for his time and wisdom; Rebecca Nathan, my wonderful executive assistant, who has put in more overtime hours than I hope she ever counts; my Phoenix staff, especially Ann Junker and Nancy Fikes, for the big launch; Dave Sime and all of the personalities who were kind enough to allow us to use their profiles and anecdotes; super-agent Mel Berger, and Irene Webb and Aames Cushing of the William Morris office; and last but not least, Rick Ridgeway, who helped me write this book. Rick is not only a world-class mountain climber, adventurer, and author but also, and more important, a world-class human being.

INDEX

O

Oat bran, 28–29
Oatmeal. *See* Oatmeal Victory
     Breakfast, The
Oatmeal Victory Breakfast,
     The, 27–30, 177, 178–179
Obesity, problems of, 4–6
Oils, 31, 194, 211–214, 226.
     See also Fats
Olive oil, 212
120-Year Diet, The (Walford),
     11
Outdoor adventure sports, 148–
     149
Overweight, problems of, 4–6

P

Page, Satchel, 248
Pain and exercise, 118–119
Palm oil, 31, 194, 208, 212
Palmer, Jim, 16, 75–77, 250
Pasta, 71–72, 225, 226
Payne, Larry, 116–117
Pay-Off Crunch, 124–125, 126
Pectin, 91–92
Phoenix Baptist Hospital, 8
Phoenix Children's Hospital, 8
*Physicians and Sportsmedicine
     Magazine* study (exercise),
     102
Pigging out, 228–229, 238–239
Plaque, 194, 208
Popcorn, 92

Posture, 132–134, 242
Potatoes, 77, 80–81, 191
Preservatives, 209. *See also* Salt
President's Council on Physical
     Fitness and Sports study
     (kids), 246
Pritikin program, 15, 136
Protein, 42, 56–59, 190
Protein Salad, 62
Pulse rate, 167–168, 198

R

Racquetball, 147
RDA, 56–57
Recipes. *See* Meal plans
Recommended Dietary Allow-
     ance (RDA), 56–57
Rectal cancer, 4
Red meat. *See* Meat
Report on Nutrition and Health
     (1988), 4, 15, 190, 249
Restaurants, eating in, 8, 55–
     56, 59, 79, 222–228
Rice, 75, 191
Ridgeway, Rick, 41, 94
Riley, Chris, 36–37
Riley, Pat, 38–39, 146
Roast Chicken, 76–77
Rockefeller University study
     (breakfast), 45
Rotation Diet, 12
Running, 116, 143, 146–147,
     246